D0592298

THE PENGUIN SHAKESPEARE

The Narrative Poems

Edited by G. B. Harrison

Two shillings and sixpence

PENGUIN BOOKS

THE PENGUIN SHAKESPEARE
EDITED FROM THE ORIGINAL TEXT
BY G. B. HARRISON
B 37
THE NARRATIVE POEMS

WILLIAM SHAKESPEARE
THE NARRATIVE
POEMS

WITH AN EPILOGUE TO THE LAST VOLUME OF
THE PENGUIN SHAKESPEARE
BY G. B. HARRISON

PENGUIN BOOKS

Penguin Books Ltd, Harmondsworth, Middlesex
AUSTRALIA: Penguin Books Pty Ltd, 762 Whitehorse Road
Mitcham, Victoria

—

This edition first published 1959

The portraits on the cover and on the title page
were engraved by Reynolds Stone

—

Made and printed in Great Britain
by Wyman & Sons Ltd,
London Fakenham and Reading

CONTENTS

THE WORKS OF SHAKESPEARE

PLAYS

APPROXIMATE DATE		FIRST PRINTED
Before 1594	HENRY VI *three parts*	Folio 1623
	RICHARD III	1597
	TITUS ANDRONICUS	1594
	LOVE'S LABOUR'S LOST	1598
	THE TWO GENTLEMEN OF VERONA	Folio
	THE COMEDY OF ERRORS	Folio
	THE TAMING OF THE SHREW	Folio
1594–1597	ROMEO AND JULIET (*pirated* 1597)	1599
	A MIDSUMMER NIGHT'S DREAM	1600
	RICHARD II	1597
	KING JOHN	Folio
	THE MERCHANT OF VENICE	1600
1597–1600	HENRY IV *part i*	1598
	HENRY IV *part ii*	1600
	HENRY V (*pirated* 1600)	Folio
	MUCH ADO ABOUT NOTHING	1600
	MERRY WIVES OF WINDSOR (*pirated* 1602)	Folio
	AS YOU LIKE IT	Folio
	JULIUS CAESAR	Folio
	TROYLUS AND CRESSIDA	1609
1601–1608	HAMLET (*pirated* 1603)	1604
	TWELFTH NIGHT	Folio
	MEASURE FOR MEASURE	Folio
	ALL'S WELL THAT ENDS WELL	Folio
	OTHELLO	1622
	LEAR	1608
	MACBETH	Folio
	TIMON OF ATHENS	Folio
	ANTHONY AND CLEOPATRA	Folio
	CORIOLANUS	Folio
After 1608	PERICLES (*omitted from the Folio*)	1609
	CYMBELINE	Folio
	THE WINTER'S TALE	Folio
	THE TEMPEST	Folio
	HENRY VIII	Folio

POEMS

DATES UNKNOWN		
	VENUS AND ADONIS	1593
	THE RAPE OF LUCRECE	1594
	SONNETS A LOVER'S COMPLAINT }	1609
	THE PHŒNIX AND THE TURTLE	1601

WILLIAM SHAKESPEARE

William Shakespeare was born at Stratford upon Avon in April, 1564. He was the third child, and eldest son, of John Shakespeare and Mary Arden. His father was one of the most prosperous men of Stratford, who held in turn the chief offices in the town. His mother was of gentle birth, the daughter of Robert Arden of Wilmcote. In December, 1582, Shakespeare married Ann Hathaway, daughter of a farmer of Shottery, near Stratford; their first child Susanna was baptized on May 6, 1583, and twins, Hamnet and Judith, on February 22, 1585. Little is known of Shakespeare's early life; but it is unlikely that a writer who dramatized such an incomparable range and variety of human kinds and experiences should have spent his early manhood entirely in placid pursuits in a country town. There is one tradition, not universally accepted, that he fled from Stratford because he was in trouble for deer stealing, and had fallen foul of Sir Thomas Lucy, the local magnate; another that he was for some time a schoolmaster.

From 1592 onwards the records are much fuller. In March, 1592, the Lord Strange's players produced a new play at the Rose Theatre called *Harry the Sixth*, which was very successful, and was probably the *First Part of Henry VI*. In the autumn of 1592 Robert Greene, the best known of the professional writers, as he was dying wrote a letter to three fellow writers in which he warned them against the ingratitude of players in general, and in particular against an ʻupstart crowʼ who ʻsupposes he is as much able to bombast out a blank verse as the best of you: and being an absolute Johannes Factotum is in his own conceit the only Shake-scene in a country.ʼ This is the first reference to

Shakespeare, and the whole passage suggests that Shakespeare had become suddenly famous as a playwright. At this time Shakespeare was brought into touch with Edward Alleyne the great tragedian, and Christopher Marlowe, whose thundering parts of Tamburlaine, the Jew of Malta, and Dr Faustus Alleyne was acting, as well as Hieronimo, the hero of Kyd's *Spanish Tragedy*, the most famous of all Elizabethan plays.

In April, 1593, Shakespeare published his poem *Venus and Adonis*, which was dedicated to the young Earl of Southampton: it was a great and lasting success, and was reprinted nine times in the next few years. In May, 1594, his second poem, *The Rape of Lucrece*, was also dedicated to Southampton.

There was little playing in 1593, for the theatres were shut during a severe outbreak of the plague; but in the autumn of 1594, when the plague ceased, the playing companies were reorganized, and Shakespeare became a sharer in the Lord Chamberlain's company who went to play in the Theatre in Shoreditch. During these months Marlowe and Kyd had died. Shakespeare was thus for a time without a rival. He had already written the three parts of *Henry VI*, *Richard III*, *Titus Andronicus*, *The Two Gentlemen of Verona*, *Love's Labour's Lost*, *The Comedy of Errors*, and *The Taming of the Shrew*. Soon afterwards he wrote the first of his greater plays – *Romeo and Juliet* – and he followed this success in the next three years with *A Midsummer Night's Dream*, *Richard II*, and *The Merchant of Venice*. The two parts of *Henry IV*, introducing Falstaff, the most popular of all his comic characters, were written in 1597–8.

The company left the Theatre in 1597 owing to disputes over a renewal of the ground lease, and went to play at the

Curtain in the same neighbourhood. The disputes continued throughout 1598, and at Christmas the players settled the matter by demolishing the old Theatre and re-erecting a new playhouse on the South bank of the Thames, near Southwark Cathedral. This playhouse was named the Globe. The expenses of the new building were shared by the chief members of the Company, including Shakespeare, who was now a man of some means. In 1596 he had bought New Place, a large house in the centre of Stratford, for £60, and through his father purchased a coat-of-arms from the Heralds, which was the official recognition that he and his family were gentlefolk.

By the summer of 1598 Shakespeare was recognized as the greatest of English dramatists. Booksellers were printing his more popular plays, at times even in pirated or stolen versions, and he received a remarkable tribute from a young writer named Francis Meres, in his book *Palladis Tamia*. In a long catalogue of English authors Meres gave Shakespeare more prominence than any other writer, and mentioned by name twelve of his plays.

Shortly before the Globe was opened, Shakespeare had completed the cycle of plays dealing with the whole story of the Wars of the Roses with *Henry V*. It was followed by *As You Like It*, and *Julius Caesar*, the first of the maturer tragedies. In the next three years he wrote *Troylus and Cressida*, *The Merry Wives of Windsor*, *Hamlet*, and *Twelfth Night*.

On March 24, 1603, Queen Elizabeth I died. The company had often performed before her, but they found her successor a far more enthusiastic patron. One of the first acts of King James was to take over the company and to promote them to be his own servants, so that henceforward they were known as the King's Men. They acted now very frequently at Court, and prospered accordingly. In the early years of the reign Shakespeare wrote the more sombre comedies, *All's Well that Ends Well*, and *Measure for Measure*, which were followed by *Othello, Macbeth*, and *King Lear*. Then he returned to Roman themes with *Antony and Cleopatra* and *Coriolanus*.

Since 1601 Shakespeare had been writing less, and there were now a number of rival dramatists who were introducing new styles of drama, particularly Ben Jonson (whose first successful comedy, *Every Man in his Humour*, was acted by Shakespeare's company in 1598), Chapman, Dekker, Marston, and Beaumont and Fletcher who began to write in 1607. In 1608 the King's Men acquired a second playhouse, an indoor private theatre in the fashionable quarter of the Blackfriars. At private theatres, plays were performed indoors; the prices charged were higher than in the public playhouses, and the audience consequently was more select. Shakespeare seems to have retired from the stage about this time: his name does not occur in the various lists of players after 1607. Henceforward he lived for the most part at Stratford, where he was regarded as one of the most important citizens. He still wrote a few plays, and he tried his hand at the new form of tragi-comedy – a play with tragic incidents but a happy ending – which Beaumont and Fletcher had popularized. He wrote four of these – *Pericles, Cymbeline, The Winter's Tale*, and *The Tempest*, which was acted at Court in 1611. For the last four years of his life he lived in retirement. His son Hamnet had died in 1596: his two daughters were now married. Shakespeare died at Stratford upon Avon on April 23, 1616, and was buried in the chancel of the church, before the high altar. Shortly afterwards a memorial which still exists, with a portrait bust, was set up on the North wall. His wife survived him.

THE POEMS

1. *Venus and Adonis*

Venus and Adonis was entered in the Stationers' Register on
18 April 1593: 'xviii° Aprilis. Richard Feild Assigned ouer
to master Harrison senior 25 Junii 1594. Entred for his
copie under thandes of the Archbisshop of Canterbury and
master warden Stirrop, a booke intituled, Venus and
Adonis, vj^d.' The first edition followed soon afterward,
with the title page: *VENUS AND ADONIS/Vilia miretur
vulgus: mihi flauus Apollo/Pocula Castalia plena ministret
aqua. London. Imprinted by Richard Field, and are to be sold at
the signe of the white Greyhound in Paules Church-yard. 1593.*
Richard Field, the printer, who had originally come from
Stratford-on-Avon, was a man of good standing in the
printing trade. The volume was finely printed in good,
large type, and was obviously intended for the best class of
reader.

Venus and Adonis is one of several poems written in the
1590s in which the physical attractions of a young man are
stressed. It was a very popular work, and though early
copies are now excessively rare, examples of editions
printed in 1594, 1596, 1599 (2), 1602 (3), as well as undated
fragments, survive. There are many references to the poem,
which was much quoted; in *England's Parnassus* (1600), a
collection of 'the choicest flowers of our modern poets,'
there are twenty-six quotations. Sober-minded readers,
however, regarded the poem as improper.

Venus and Adonis is written in a six-line stanza, each line
having five stresses, the rhyme scheme being ababcc. This
pattern was not common, but it had been used by Spenser

in the First Eclogue in *The Shepherd's Calendar* (1579), and also by Thomas Lodge in *Scilla's Metamorphosis* (1589).

The story of Venus's passion for Adonis was well known and often retold. Shakespeare probably first met it in Ovid's *Metamorphoses,* and he could also have taken hints from Lodge's poem. The story was told also in Spenser's *Faerie Queene* (Book III, Canto i, 34–38; 1591), in which there is given a luscious description of the Castle Joyous:

The walls were round about apparelled
With costly cloths of Arras and of Tour,
In which with cunning hand was portrayed
The love of Venus and her Paramour
The fair Adonis, turned to a flower,
A work of rare device, and wondrous wit.
First did it show the bitter baleful stour,
Which her assayed with many a fervent fit,
When first her tender heart was with his beauty smit. ....

And whilst he slept, she over him would spread
Her mantle, coloured like the starry skies,
And her soft arm lay underneath his head,
And with ambrosial kisses bathe his eyes;
And whilst he bathed, with her two crafty spies,
She secretly would search each dainty limb,
And throw into the well sweet rosemaries,
And fragrant violets, and pansies trim,
And ever with sweet nectar she did sprinkle him.

So did she steal his heedless heart away,
And joyed his love in secret unespied.
But for she saw him bent to cruel play,

To hunt the savage beast in forest wide,
Dreadful of danger, that mote him betide,
She oft and oft advis'd him to refrain
From chase of greater beasts, whose brutish pride
Mote breed him scathe unwares: but all in vain;
For who can shun the chance, that dest'ny doth ordain?

Lo, where beyond he lieth languishing,
Deadly engored of a great wild Boar,
And by his side the Goddess grovelling
Makes for him endless moan, and evermore
With her soft garment wipes away the gore,
Which stains his snowy skin with hateful hue:
But when she saw no help might him restore,
Him to a dainty flower she did transmew,
Which in that cloth was wrought, as if it lively grew.

A contemporary illustration of the story 'with cunning hand portrayed' in needlework is to be found in the Victoria and Albert Museum.

2. Lucrece

Lucrece was entered in the Stationers' Register on 9 May 1594: '9 Maij. Master Harrison Senior Entred for his copie vnder thand of Master Cawood Warden, a booke intituled the Ravyshement of Lucrece vj^d.' The poem was soon after printed with the title page: *LUCRECE. London. Printed by Richard Field, for Iohn Harrison, and are to be sold at the signe of the white Greyhound in Paules Church-yard. 1594.*

Lucrece was a handsome piece of printing, in a similar style to *Venus and Adonis*, which was also the work of

Richard Field. It was a popular success and went into several editions. Copies exist dated 1598, 1600 (2), and 1607; two other early editions, undated, are also known. The poem was much admired, especially by the graver kind of reader, and thirty-nine quotations from it are included in *England's Parnassus*.

The story of the fate of Lucrece was part of Roman legend and was told in Latin by Livy in his Roman history and by Ovid in his *Fasti*. Lucrece also appears among the heroines in Chaucer's *Legend of Good Women* where her tale is told at some length. No story was more popular in Elizabethan times, and references to it are very common.

The poem is written in the metre known as rhyme royal, which consists of stanzas of seven lines, rhymed ababbcc, each line bearing five stresses. This metre had been used by Chaucer and was common in the fifteenth and sixteenth centuries. It was also used by Samuel Daniel in *The Complaint of Rosamond*, one of several poems written in the 1590s which relate the sad fate of some distressed lady of legend.

3. *The Phoenix and Turtle*

In 1601 a little collection of poems was published with the title *Love's Martyr: Or, Rosalins Complaint. Allegorically shadowing the truth of Loue, in the constant Fate of the Phoenix and Turtle. A Poeme interlaced with much varietie and raritie; now first translated out of the venerable Italian Torquato Caeliano, by Robert Chester. With the true legend of famous King Arthur, the last of the nine Worthies, being the first Essay of a new Brytish Poet: collected out of diuerse Authenticall Records. To these are added some new compositions, of seuerall moderne Writers whose names are subscribed to their seuerall workes, upon the first subiect: viz. the Phoenix and Turtle. Mar: – Mutare dominum non potest liber notus. London Imprinted for E. B. 1601.* These 'new compositions' are thus prefaced:

'Hereafter follow diverse Poeticall Essaies on the former Subiect; viz: the Turtle and Phoenix. Done by the best and chiefest of our moderne writers, with their names subscribed to their particular works: neuer before extant. And (now first) consecrated by them all generally, to the loue and merite of the true-noble Knight, Sir John Salisburie. Dignum laude virum Musa vetat mori. Anchora Spei. MDCI.'

The writers' names are Shakespeare, John Marston, George Chapman, and Benjamin Jonson, as well as 'Chorus Vatum' and 'Ignoto'.

Shakespeare's little contribution to the collection is difficult and enigmatical, and no one has yet offered any satisfactory interpretation of its inner meaning. On the surface it celebrates, in obscure symbolism, the spiritual union of the Phoenix (true love) and the Turtledove (constancy). It is likely, however, that the poem has other and inner meanings that were well understood by the small circle of readers for whom it was originally intended. Until these persons and events are discovered, *The Phoenix and the Turtle* will remain an enigma.

The texts of the Poems have been closely reproduced from the original quartos, following the principles laid down for the Penguin Shakespeare. Spelling and use of capital letters have been conservatively modernized, but the original punctuation, intended to point the text for reading aloud, has been followed, except for a very few instances where it seemed obviously wrong and confusing.

The Poems

Venus and Adonis

Vilia miretur vulgus; mihi flavus Apollo
Pocula Castalia plena ministret aqua

To the Right Honourable

HENRY WRIOTHESLEY

*Earl of Southampton, and
Baron of Titchfield*

RIGHT HONOURABLE, I know not how I
shall offend in dedicating my unpolish'd lines
to your Lordship, nor how the world will cen-
sure me for choosing so strong a prop to support so weak a burthen, only if your Honour
seem but pleased, I account myself highly
praised, and vow to take advantage of all idle
hours, till I have honoured you with some
graver labour. But if the first heir of my invention prove deformed, I shall be sorry it had
so noble a godfather: and never after ear so
barren a land, for fear it yield me still so bad a
harvest, I leave it to your Honourable survey,
and your Honour to your heart's content,
which I wish may always answer your own
wish, and the world's hopeful expectation.

Your Honours in all duty

WILLIAM SHAKESPEARE

VENUS AND ADONIS

Even as the sun with purple-colour'd face,
Had ta'en his last leave of the weeping morn,
Rose-cheek'd Adonis hied him to the chase,
Hunting he lov'd, but love he laugh'd to scorn:
    Sick-thoughted Venus makes amain unto him,
    And like a bold fac'd suitor 'gins to woo him.

Thrice fairer than myself, (thus she began)
The field's chief flower, sweet above compare,
Stain to all Nymphs, more lovely than a man,
More white, and red, than doves, or roses are:
    Nature that made thee with herself at strife,
    Saith that the world hath ending with thy life.

Vouchsafe thou wonder to alight thy steed,
And rein his proud head to the saddle bow,
If thou wilt deign this favour, for thy meed
A thousand honey secrets shalt thou know:
    Here come and sit, where never serpent hisses,
    And being set, I'll smother thee with kisses.

And yet not cloy thy lips with loath'd satiety,
But rather famish them amid their plenty,
Making them red, and pale, with fresh variety:
Ten kisses short as one, one long as twenty:
    A summer's day will seem an hour but short,
    Being wasted in such time-beguiling sport.

With this she seizeth on his sweating palm,
The precedent of pith, and livelihood,
And, trembling in her passion, calls it balm,
Earth's sovereign salve, to do a goddess good,
    Being so enrag'd, desire doth lend her force,
    Courageously to pluck him from his horse.

Over one arm the lusty courser's rein,
Under her other was the tender boy,
Who blush'd, and pouted in a dull disdain,
With leaden appetite, unapt to toy,
   She red, and hot, as coals of glowing fire,
   He red for shame, but frosty in desire.

The studded bridle in a ragged bough,
Nimbly she fastens, (oh, how quick is love!)
The steed is stalled up, and even now,
To tie the rider she begins to prove:
   Backward she push'd him, as she would be thrust,
   And govern'd him in strength though not in lust.

So soon was she along, as he was down,
Each leaning on their elbows and their hips:
Now doth she stroke his cheek, now doth he frown,
And 'gins to chide, but soon she stops his lips,
   And kissing speaks, with lustful language broken,
   If thou wilt chide, thy lips shall never open.

He burns with bashful shame, she with her tears
Doth quench the maiden burning of his cheeks,
Then with her windy sighs, and golden hairs,
To fan, and blow them dry again she seeks.
   He saith, she is immodest, blames her miss,
   What follows more, she murthers with a kiss.

Even as an empty Eagle sharp by fast,
Tires with her beak on feathers, flesh, and bone,
Shaking her wings, devouring all in haste,
Till either gorge be stuff'd, or prey be gone:
   Even so she kiss'd his brow, his cheek, his chin,
   And where she ends, she doth anew begin.

Forc'd to content, but never to obey,
Panting he lies, and breatheth in her face.
She feedeth on the steam, as on a prey,
And calls it heavenly moisture, air of grace,
    Wishing her cheeks were gardens full of flowers,
    So they were dew'd with such distilling showers.

Look how a bird lies tangled in a net,
So fasten'd in her arms Adonis lies,
Pure shame and aw'd resistance made him fret,
Which bred more beauty in his angry eyes:
    Rain added to a river that is rank,
    Perforce will force it overflow the bank.

Still she entreats, and prettily entreats,
For to a pretty ear she tunes her tale.
Still is he sullen, still he lours and frets,
'Twixt crimson shame, and anger ashy pale,
    Being red she loves him best, and being white,
    Her best is better'd with a more delight.

Look how he can, she cannot choose but love,
And by her fair immortal hand she swears,
From his soft bosom never to remove,
Till he take truce with her contending tears,
    Which long have rain'd, making her cheeks all wet,
    And one sweet kiss shall pay this comptless debt.

Upon this promise did he raise his chin,
Like a divedapper peering through a wave,
Who being look'd on, ducks as quickly in:
So offers he to give what she did crave,
    But when her lips were ready for his pay,
    He winks, and turns his lips another way.

Never did passenger in summer's heat,
More thirst for drink, than she for this good turn,
Her help she sees, but help she cannot get,
She bathes in water, yet her fire must burn:
    Oh pity gan she cry, flint-hearted boy,
    'Tis but a kiss I beg, why art thou coy?

I have been woo'd as I entreat thee now,
Even by the stern, and direful god of war,
Whose sinewy neck in battle ne'er did bow,
Who conquers where he comes in every jar,
    Yet hath he been my captive, and my slave,
    And begg'd for that which thou unask'd shalt have.

Over my altars hath he hong his lance,
His batter'd shield, his uncontrolled crest,
And for my sake hath learn'd to sport, and dance,
To toy, to wanton, dally, smile, and jest,
    Scorning his churlish drum, and ensign red,
    Making my arms his field, his tent my bed.

Thus he that over-rul'd, I over-sway'd,
Leading him prisoner in a red rose chain,
Strong-temper'd steel his stronger strength obeyed.
Yet was he servile to my coy disdain,
    Oh be not proud, nor brag not of thy might,
    For mastering her that foil'd the god of fight.

Touch but my lips with those fair lips of thine,
Though mine be not so fair, yet are they red,
The kiss shall be thine own as well as mine,
What see'st thou in the ground? hold up thy head,
    Look in mine eyeballs, there thy beauty lies,
    Then why not lips on lips, since eyes in eyes?

Art thou asham'd to kiss? then wink again,
And I will wink, so shall the day seem night.
Love keeps his revels where there are but twain:
Be bold to play, our sport is not in sight,
  These blue-vein'd violets whereon we lean,
  Never can blab, nor know not what we mean.

The tender spring upon thy tempting lip,
Shews thee unripe; yet mayst thou well be tasted,
Make use of time, let not advantage slip,
Beauty within itself should not be wasted,
  Fair flowers that are not gather'd in their prime,
  Rot, and consume themselves in little time.

Were I hard-favour'd, foul, or wrinkled old,
Ill-nurtur'd, crooked, churlish, harsh in voice,
O'erworn, despised, rheumatic, and cold,
Thick-sighted, barren, lean, and lacking juice;
  Then mightst thou pause, for then I were not for thee,
  But having no defects, why dost abhor me?

Thou canst not see one wrinkle in my brow,
Mine eyes are grey, and bright, and quick in turning:
My beauty as the spring doth yearly grow,
My flesh is soft, and plump, my marrow burning,
  My smooth moist hand, were it with thy hand felt,
  Would in thy palm dissolve, or seem to melt.

Bid me discourse, I will enchant thine ear,
Or like a Fairy, trip upon the green,
Or like a Nymph, with long dishevell'd hair,
Dance on the sands, and yet no footing seen.
  Love is a spirit all compact of fire,
  Not gross to sink, but light, and will aspire.

Witness this primrose bank whereon I lie,
These forceless flowers like sturdy trees support me:
Two strengthless doves will draw me through the sky,
From morn till night, even where I list to sport me.
　　Is love so light sweet boy, and may it be,
　　That thou should think it heavy unto thee?

Is thine own heart to thine own face affected?
Can thy right hand seize love upon thy left?
Then woo thyself, be of thyself rejected:
Steal thine own freedom, and complain on theft.
　　Narcissus so himself himself forsook,
　　And died to kiss his shadow in the brook.

Torches are made to light, jewels to wear,
Dainties to taste, fresh beauty for the use,
Herbs for their smell, and sappy plants to bear.
Things growing to themselves, are growth's abuse,
　　Seeds spring from seeds, and beauty breedeth beauty,
　　Thou wast begot, to get it is thy duty.

Upon the earth's increase why shouldst thou feed,
Unless the earth with thy increase be fed?
By law of nature thou art bound to breed,
That thine may live, when thou thyself art dead:
　　And so in spite of death thou dost survive,
　　In that thy likeness still is left alive.

By this the love-sick Queen began to sweat,
For where they lay the shadow had forsook them,
And Titan tired in the midday heat,
With burning eye did hotly over-look them,
　　Wishing Adonis had his team to guide,
　　So he were like him, and by Venus' side.

And now Adonis with a lazy sprite,
And with a heavy, dark, disliking eye,
His louring brows o'erwhelming his fair sight,
Like misty vapours when they blot the sky,
    Souring his cheeks, cries, fie, no more of love,
    The sun doth burn my face I must remove.

Ay, me, (quoth Venus) young, and so unkind,
What bare excuses mak'st thou to be gone?
I'll sigh celestial breath, whose gentle wind,
Shall cool the heat of this descending sun:
    I'll make a shadow for thee of my hairs,
    If they burn too, I'll quench them with my tears.

The sun that shines from heaven, shines but warm,
And lo I lie between that sun, and thee:
The heat I have from thence doth little harm,
Thine eye darts forth the fire that burneth me,
    And were I not immortal, life were done,
    Between this heavenly, and earthly sun.

Art thou obdurate, flinty, hard as steel?
Nay more than flint, for stone at rain relenteth:
Art thou a woman's son and canst not feel
What 'tis to love, how want of love tormenteth?
    O had thy mother borne so hard a mind,
    She had not brought forth thee, but died unkind.

What am I that thou shouldst contemn me this?
Or what great danger, dwells upon my suit?
What were thy lips the worse for one poor kiss?
Speak, fair, but speak fair words, or else be mute:
    Give me one kiss, I'll give it thee again,
    And one for intrest, if thou wilt have twain.

Fie, lifeless picture, cold, and senseless stone,
Well painted idol, image dull, and dead,
Statue contenting but the eye alone,
Thing like a man, but of no woman bred:
    Thou art no man, though of a man's complexion,
    For men will kiss even by their own direction.

This said, impatience chokes her pleading tongue,
And swelling passion doth provoke a pause,
Red cheeks, and fiery eyes blaze forth her wrong:
Being Judge in love, she cannot right her cause.
    And now she weeps, and now she fain would speak
    And now her sobs do her intendments break.

Sometime she shakes her head, and then his hand,
Now gazeth she on him, now on the ground;
Sometime her arms infold him like a band,
She would, he will not in her arms be bound:
    And when from thence he struggles to be gone,
    She locks her lily fingers one in one.

Fondling, she saith, since I have hemm'd thee here
Within the circuit of this ivory pale,
I'll be a park, and thou shalt be my dear:
Feed where thou wilt, on mountain, or in dale;
    Graze on my lips, and if those hills be dry,
    Stray lower, where the pleasant fountains lie.

Within this limit is relief enough,
Sweet bottom grass, and high delightful plain,
Round rising hillocks, brakes obscure, and rough,
To shelter thee from tempest, and from rain:
    Then be my dear, since I am such a park,
    No dog shall rouse thee, though a thousand bark.

At this Adonis smiles as in disdain,
That in each cheek appears a pretty dimple;
Love made those hollows, if himself were slain,
He might be buried in a tomb so simple,
    Foreknowing well, if there he came to lie,
    Why there love liv'd, and there he could not die.

These lovely caves, these round enchanting pits,
Open'd their mouths to swallow Venus' liking:
Being mad before, how doth she now for wits?
Struck dead at first, what needs a second striking?
    Poor Queen of love, in thine own law forlorn,
    To love a cheek that smiles at thee in scorn.

Now which way shall she turn? what shall she say?
Her words are done, her woes the more increasing,
The time is spent, her object will away,
And from her twining arms doth urge releasing:
    Pity she cries, some favour, some remorse,
    Away he springs, and hasteth to his horse.

But lo from forth a copse that neighbours by,
A breeding Jennet, lusty, young, and proud,
Adonis' trampling Courser doth espy:
And forth she rushes, snorts, and neighs aloud.
    The strong-neck'd steed being tied unto a tree,
    Breaketh his rein, and to her straight goes he.

Imperiously he leaps, he neighs, he bounds,
And now his woven girths he breaks asunder,
The bearing earth with his hard hoof he wounds,
Whose hollow womb resounds like heaven's thunder,
    The iron bit he crusheth 'tween his teeth,
    Controlling what he was controlled with.

His ears up prick'd, his braided hanging mane
Upon his compass'd crest now stand on end,
His nostrils drink the air, and forth again
As from a furnace, vapours doth he send:
　　His eye which scornfully glisters like fire,
　　Shows his hot courage, and his high desire.

Sometime he trots, as if he told the steps,
With gentle majesty, and modest pride,
Anon he rears upright, curvets, and leaps,
As who should say, lo thus my strength is tried.
　　And this I do, to captivate the eye,
　　Of the fair breeder that is standing by.

What recketh he his rider's angry stir,
His flattering holla, or his stand, I say,
What cares he now, for curb, or pricking spur,
For rich caparisons, or trappings gay:
　　He sees his love, and nothing else he sees,
　　For nothing else with his proud sight agrees.

Look when a Painter would surpass the life,
In limning out a well proportion'd steed,
His Art with Nature's workmanship at strife,
As if the dead the living should exceed:
　　So did this Horse excel a common one,
　　In shape, in courage, colour, pace and bone.

Round hoof'd, short jointed, fetlocks shag, and long,
Broad breast, full eye, small head, and nostril wide,
High crest, short ears, straight legs, and passing strong,
Thin mane, thick tail, broad buttock, tender hide:
　　Look what a Horse should have, he did not lack,
　　Save a proud rider on so proud a back.

Sometime he scuds far off, and there he stares,
Anon he starts, at stirring of a feather:
To bid the wind a base he now prepares,
And whe'er he run, or fly, they know not whether:
  For through his mane, and tail, the high wind sings,
  Fanning the hairs, who wave like feather'd wings.

He looks upon his love, and neighs unto her,
She answers him, as if she knew his mind,
Being proud as females are, to see him woo her,
She puts on outward strangeness, seems unkind:
  Spurns at his love, and scorns the heat he feels,
  Beating his kind embracements with her heels.

Then like a melancholy malcontent,
He vails his tail that like a falling plume,
Cool shadow to his melting buttock lent,
He stamps, and bites the poor flies in his fume:
  His love perceiving how he was enrag'd,
  Grew kinder, and his fury was assuag'd.

His testy master goeth about to take him,
When lo the unback'd breeder full of fear,
Jealous of catching, swiftly doth forsake him,
With her the Horse, and left Adonis there:
  As they were mad unto the wood they hie them,
  Outstripping crows, that strive to overfly them.

All swoln with chafing, down Adonis sits,
Banning his boisterous, and unruly beast;
And now the happy season once more fits
That lovesick love, by pleading may be blest:
  For lovers say, the heart hath treble wrong,
  When it is barr'd the aidance of the tongue.

An oven that is stopp'd, or river stay'd,
Burneth more hotly, swelleth with more rage:
So of concealed sorrow may be said,
Free vent of words love's fire doth assuage,
　　But when the heart's attorney once is mute,
　　The client breaks, as desperate in his suit.

He sees her coming, and begins to glow:
Even as a dying coal revives with wind,
And with his bonnet hides his angry brow,
Looks on the dull earth with disturbed mind:
　　Taking no notice that she is so nigh,
　　For all askance he holds her in his eye.

O what a sight it was wistly to view,
How she came stealing to the wayward boy,
To note the fighting conflict of her hue,
How white and red, each other did destroy:
　　But now her cheek was pale, and by and by
　　It flash'd forth fire, as lightning from the sky.

Now was she just before him as he sat,
And like a lowly lover down she kneels,
With one fair hand she heaveth up his hat,
Her other tender hand his fair cheek feels:
　　His tenderer cheek, receives her soft hand's print,
　　As apt, as new fall'n snow takes any dint.

O what a war of looks was then between them,
Her eyes petitioners to his eyes suing,
His eyes saw her eyes, as they had not seen them,
Her eyes woo'd still, his eyes disdain'd the wooing:
　　And all this dumb play had his acts made plain,
　　With tears which Chorus-like her eyes did rain.

Full gently now she takes him by the hand,
A lily prison'd in a gaol of snow,
Or ivory in an alablaster band,
So white a friend, engirts so white a foe:
    This beauteous combat wilful, and unwilling,
    Show'd like two silver doves that sit a-billing.

Once more the engine of her thoughts began,
O fairest mover on this mortal round,
Would thou wert as I am, and I a man,
My heart all whole as thine, thy heart my wound,
    For one sweet look thy help I would assure thee,
    Though nothing but my body's bane would cure thee.

Give me my hand (saith he), why dost thou feel it?
Give me my heart (saith she), and thou shalt have it.
O give it me lest thy hard heart do steel it,
And being steel'd, soft sighs can never grave it.
    Then love's deep groans, I never shall regard,
    Because Adonis' heart hath made mine hard.

For shame he cries, let go, and let me go,
My day's delight is past, my horse is gone,
And 'tis your fault I am bereft him so,
I pray you hence, and leave me here alone,
    For all my mind, my thought, my busy care,
    Is how to get my palfrey from the mare.

Thus she replies, thy palfrey as he should,
Welcomes the warm approach of sweet desire,
Affection is a coal that must be cool'd,
Else suffer'd it will set the heart on fire,
    The sea hath bounds, but deep desire hath none,
    Therefore no marvel though thy horse be gone.

B

How like a jade he stood tied to the tree,
Servilely master'd with a leathern rein,
But when he saw his love, his youth's fair fee,
He held such petty bondage in disdain:
    Throwing the base thong from his bending crest,
    Enfranchising his mouth, his back, his breast.

Who sees his true-love in her naked bed,
Teaching the sheets a whiter hue than white,
But when his glutton eye so full hath fed,
His other agents aim at like delight?
    Who is so faint that dares not be so bold,
    To touch the fire the weather being cold?

Let me excuse thy courser gentle boy,
And learn of him I heartily beseech thee,
To take advantage on presented joy,
Though I were dumb, yet his proceedings teach thee:
    O learn to love, the lesson is but plain,
    And once made perfect, never lost again.

I know not love (quoth he) nor will not know it,
Unless it be a boar, and then I chase it,
'Tis much to borrow, and I will not owe it,
My love to love, is love, but to disgrace it,
    For I have heard, it is a life in death,
    That laughs and weeps, and all but with a breath.

Who wears a garment shapeless and unfinish'd?
Who plucks the bud before one leaf put forth?
If springing things be any jot diminish'd,
They wither in their prime, prove nothing worth,
    The colt that's back'd and burthen'd being young,
    Loseth his pride, and never waxeth strong.

You hurt my hand with wringing, let us part,
And leave this idle theme, this bootless chat,
Remove your siege from my unyielding heart,
To love's alarms it will not ope the gate,
  Dismiss your vows, your feigned tears, your flattery,
  For where a heart is hard they make no battery.

What canst thou talk (quoth she) hast thou a tongue?
O would thou hadst not, or I had no hearing,
Thy mermaid's voice hath done me double wrong,
I had my load before, now press'd with bearing,
  Melodious discord, heavenly tune harsh sounding,
  Ear's deep sweet music, and heart's deep sore wounding.

Had I no eyes but ears, my ears would love,
That inward beauty and invisible,
Or were I deaf, thy outward parts would move
Each part in me, that were but sensible,
  Though neither eyes, nor ears, to hear nor see,
  Yet should I be in love, by touching thee.

Say that the sense of feeling were bereft me,
And that I could not see, nor hear, nor touch,
And nothing but the very smell were left me,
Yet would my love to thee be still as much,
  For from the stillitory of thy face excelling,
  Comes breath perfum'd, that breedeth love by smelling.

But o what banquet wert thou to the taste,
Being nurse, and feeder of the other four,
Would they not wish the feast might ever last,
And bid suspicion double-lock the door;
  Lest jealousy that sour unwelcome guest,
  Should by his stealing in disturb the feast?

Once more the ruby-colour'd portal open'd,
Which to his speech did honey passage yield,
Like a red morn that ever yet betoken'd,
Wrack to the sea-man, tempest to the field:
   Sorrow to shepherds, woe unto the birds,
   Gusts, and foul flaws, to herdmen, and to herds.

This ill presage advisedly she marketh,
Even as the wind is hush'd before it raineth:
Or as the wolf doth grin before he barketh:
Or as the berry breaks before it staineth:
   Or like the deadly bullet of a gun:
   His meaning struck her ere his words begun.

And at his look she flatly falleth down,
For looks kill love, and love by looks reviveth,
A smile recures the wounding of a frown,
But blessed bankrout that by love so thriveth.
   The silly boy believing she is dead,
   Claps her pale cheek, till clapping makes it red.

And all amaz'd, brake off his late intent,
For sharply he did think to reprehend her,
Which cunning love did wittily prevent,
Fair fall the wit that can so well defend her:
   For on the grass she lies as she were slain,
   Till his breath breatheth life in her again.

He wrings her nose, he strikes her on the cheeks,
He bends her fingers, holds her pulses hard,
He chafes her lips, a thousand ways he seeks,
To mend the hurt, that his unkindness marr'd,
   He kisses her, and she by her good will,
   Will never rise, so he will kiss her still.

The night of sorrow now is turn'd to day,
Her two blue windows faintly she upheaveth,
Like the fair sun when in his fresh array,
He cheers the morn, and all the earth relieveth:
  And as the bright sun glorifies the sky:
  So is her face illumin'd with her eye.

Whose beams upon his hairless face are fix'd,
As if from thence they borrow'd all their shine,
Were never four such lamps, together mix'd,
Had not his clouded with his brow's repine.
  But hers, which through the crystal tears gave light,
  Shone like the Moon in water seen by night.

O where am I (quoth she), in earth or heaven,
Or in the Ocean drench'd, or in the fire:
What hour is this, or morn, or weary even,
Do I delight to die or life desire?
  But now I liv'd, and life was death's annoy.
  But now I died, and death was lively joy.

O thou didst kill me, kill me once again,
Thy eyes' shrewd tutor, that hard heart of thine,
Hath taught them scornful tricks, and such disdain,
That they have murdred this poor heart of mine,
  And these mine eyes true leaders to their queen,
  But for thy piteous lips no more had seen.

Long may they kiss each other for this cure,
Oh never let their crimson liveries wear,
And as they last, their verdure still endure,
To drive infection from the dangerous year:
  That the star-gazers having writ on death,
  May say, the plague is banish'd by thy breath.

Pure lips, sweet seals in my soft lips imprinted,
What bargains may I make still to be sealing?
To sell myself I can be well contented,
So thou wilt buy, and pay, and use good dealing,
    Which purchase if thou make, for fear of slips,
    Set thy seal manual, on my wax-red lips.

A thousand kisses buys my heart from me,
And pay them at thy leisure, one by one,
What is ten hundred touches unto thee,
Are they not quickly told, and quickly gone?
    Say for non-payment, that the debt should double,
    Is twenty hundred kisses such a trouble?

Fair Queen (quoth he) if any love you owe me,
Measure my strangeness with my unripe years,
Before I know myself, seek not to know me,
No fisher but the ungrown fry forbears,
    The mellow plum doth fall, the green sticks fast,
    Or being early pluck'd, is sour to taste.

Look the world's comforter with weary gait,
His day's hot task hath ended in the west,
The owl (night's herald) shrieks, 'tis very late,
The sheep are gone to fold, birds to their nest,
    And coal-black clouds, that shadow heaven's light,
    Do summon us to part, and bid good night.

Now let me say good night, and so say you,
If you will say so, you shall have a kiss;
Good night (quoth she) and ere he says adieu,
The honey fee of parting tender'd is,
    Her arms do lend his neck a sweet embrace,
    Incorporate then they seem, face grows to face.

Till breathless he disjoin'd, and backward drew,
The heavenly moisture that sweet coral mouth,
Whose precious taste, her thirsty lips well knew,
Whereon they surfeit, yet complain on drouth,
   He with her plenty press'd, she faint with dearth,
   Their lips together glued, fall to the earth.

Now quick desire hath caught the yielding prey,
And glutton-like she feeds, yet never filleth,
Her lips are conquerors, his lips obey,
Paying what ransom the insulter willeth:
   Whose vulture thought doth pitch the price so high,
   That she will draw his lips' rich treasure dry.

And having felt the sweetness of the spoil,
With blindfold fury she begins to forage,
Her face doth reek, and smoke, her blood doth boil,
And careless lust stirs up a desperate courage,
   Planting oblivion, beating reason back,
   Forgetting shame's pure blush, and honour's wrack.

Hot, faint, and weary, with her hard embracing,
Like a wild bird being tam'd with too much handling,
Or as the fleet-foot roe that's tir'd with chasing,
Or like the froward infant still'd with dandling:
   He now obeys, and now no more resisteth,
   While she takes all she can, not all she listeth.

What wax so frozen but dissolves with tempering,
And yields at last to every light impression?
Things out of hope, are compass'd oft with ventring,
Chiefly in love, whose leave exceeds commission:
   Affection faints not like a pale-fac'd coward,
   But then woos best, when most his choice is froward.

When he did frown, oh had she then gave over,
Such nectar from his lips she had not suck'd,
Foul words, and frowns, must not repel a lover,
What though the rose have prickles, yet 'tis pluck'd?
　　Were beauty under twenty locks kept fast,
　　Yet love breaks through, and picks them all at last.

For pity now she can no more detain him,
The poor fool prays her that he may depart,
She is resolv'd no longer to restrain him,
Bids him farewell, and look well to her heart,
　　The which by Cupid's bow she doth protest,
　　He carries thence incaged in his breast.

Sweet boy she says, this night I'll waste in sorrow,
For my sick heart commands mine eyes to watch,
Tell me love's master, shall we meet tomorrow,
Say, shall we, shall we, wilt thou make the match?
　　He tells her no, tomorrow he intends,
　　To hunt the boar with certain of his friends.

The boar (quoth she) whereat a sudden pale,
Like lawn being spread upon the blushing rose,
Usurps her cheek, she trembles at his tale,
And on his neck her yoking arms she throws.
　　She sinketh down, still hanging by his neck,
　　He on her belly falls, she on her back.

Now is she in the very lists of love,
Her champion mounted for the hot encounter,
All is imaginary she doth prove,
He will not manage her, although he mount her,
　　That worse than Tantalus' is her annoy,
　　To clip Elysium, and to lack her joy.

Even so poor birds deceiv'd with painted grapes,
Do surfeit by the eye, and pine the maw:
Even so she languisheth in her mishaps,
As those poor birds that helpless berries saw,
    The warm effects which she in him finds missing,
    She seeks to kindle with continual kissing.

But all in vain, good Queen, it will not be,
She hath assay'd as much as may be prov'd,
Her pleading hath deserv'd a greater fee,
She's love; she loves, and yet she is not lov'd:
    Fie, fie, he says, you crush me, let me go,
    You have no reason to withhold me so.

Thou hadst been gone (quoth she) sweet boy ere this,
But that thou told'st me, thou wouldst hunt the boar,
O be advis'd, thou know'st not what it is,
With javelin's point a churlish swine to gore,
    Whose tushes never sheath'd, he whetteth still,
    Like to a mortal butcher bent to kill.

On his bow-back, he hath a battle set,
Of bristly pikes that ever threat his foes,
His eyes like glow-worms shine, when he doth fret
His snout digs sepulchres where'er he goes,
    Being mov'd he strikes, whate'er is in his way,
    And whom he strikes, his crooked tushes slay.

His brawny sides with hairy bristles armed,
Are better proof than thy spear's point can enter,
His short thick neck cannot be easily harmed,
Being ireful, on the lion he will venter,
    The thorny brambles, and embracing bushes,
    As fearful of him part, through whom he rushes.

Alas, he nought esteems that face of thine,
To which love's eyes pays tributary gazes,
Nor thy soft hands, sweet lips, and crystal eyne,
Whose full perfection all the world amazes,
    But having thee at vantage (wondrous dread!)
    Would root these beauties, as he roots the mead.

O let him keep his loathsome cabin still,
Beauty hath nought to do with such foul fiends,
Come not within his danger by thy will,
They that thrive well, take counsel of their friends,
    When thou didst name the boar, not to dissemble,
    I fear'd thy fortune, and my joints did tremble.

Didst thou not mark my face, was it not white?
Saw'st thou not signs of fear lurk in mine eye?
Grew I not faint, and fell I not down right?
Within my bosom whereon thou dost lie,
    My boding heart, pants, beats, and takes no rest,
    But like an earthquake, shakes thee on my breast.

For where love reigns, disturbing jealousy,
Doth call himself affection's sentinel,
Gives false alarms, suggesteth mutiny,
And in a peaceful hour doth cry, kill, kill,
    Distempering gentle love in his desire,
    As air, and water do abate the fire.

This sour informer, this bate-breeding spy,
This canker that eats up love's tender spring,
This carry-tale, dissentious jealousy,
That sometime true news, sometime false doth bring,
    Knocks at my heart, and whispers in mine ear,
    That if I love thee, I thy death should fear.

And more than so, presenteth to mine eye,
The picture of an angry chafing boar,
Under whose sharp fangs, on his back doth lie,
An image like thyself, all stain'd with gore,
　　Whose blood upon the fresh flowers being shed,
　　Doth make them droop with grief, and hang the head.

What should I do, seeing thee so indeed?
That tremble at th' imagination?
The thought of it doth make my faint heart bleed,
And fear doth teach it divination;
　　I prophesy thy death, my living sorrow,
　　If thou encounter with the boar tomorrow.

But if thou needs wilt hunt, be rul'd by me,
Uncouple at the timorous flying hare,
Or at the fox which lives by subtlety,
Or at the roe which no encounter dare:
　　Pursue these fearful creatures o'er the downs,
　　And on thy well-breath'd horse keep with thy hounds.

And when thou hast on foot the purblind hare,
Mark the poor wretch to over-shoot his troubles,
How he outruns the wind, and with what care,
He cranks and crosses with a thousand doubles,
　　The many musits through the which he goes,
　　Are like a labyrinth to amaze his foes.

Sometime he runs among a flock of sheep,
To make the cunning hounds mistake their smell,
And sometime where earth-delving conies keep,
To stop the loud pursuers in their yell:
　　And sometime sorteth with a herd of deer,
　　Danger deviseth shifts, wit waits on fear.

For there his smell with others being mingled,
The hot scent-snuffing hounds are driven to doubt,
Ceasing their clamorous cry, till they have singled
With much ado the cold fault cleanly out,
　　Then do they spend their mouths, echo replies,
　　As if another chase were in the skies.

By this poor Wat far off upon a hill,
Stands on his hinder-legs with listning ear,
To hearken if his foes pursue him still,
Anon their loud alarums he doth hear,
　　And now his grief may be compared well,
　　To one sore sick, that hears the passing-bell.

Then shalt thou see the dew-bedabbled wretch,
Turn, and return, indenting with the way,
Each envious briar, his weary legs do scratch,
Each shadow makes him stop, each murmur stay,
　　For misery is trodden on by many,
　　And being low, never reliev'd by any.

Lie quietly, and hear a little more,
Nay do not struggle, for thou shalt not rise,
To make thee hate the hunting of the boar,
Unlike myself thou hear'st me moralize,
　　Applying this to that, and so to so,
　　For love can comment upon every woe.

Where did I leave? no matter where (quoth he)
Leave me, and then the story aptly ends,
The night is spent; why what of that (quoth she)?
I am (quoth he) expected of my friends,
　　And now 'tis dark, and going I shall fall.
　　In night, (quoth she) desire sees best of all.

But if thou fall, o then imagine this,
The earth in love with thee, thy footing trips,
And all is but to rob thee of a kiss,
Rich preys make true men thieves: so do thy lips
    Make modest Dian, cloudy and forlorn,
    Lest she should steal a kiss and die forsworn.

Now of this dark night I perceive the reason,
Cynthia for shame, obscures her silver shine,
Till forging nature be condemn'd of treason,
For stealing moulds from heaven, that were divine,
    Wherein she fram'd thee, in high heaven's despite,
    To shame the sun by day, and her by night.

And therefore hath she brib'd the destinies,
To cross the curious workmanship of nature,
To mingle beauty with infirmities,
And pure perfection with impure defeature,
    Making it subject to the tyranny,
    Of mad mischances, and much misery.

As burning fevers, agues pale, and faint,
Life-poisoning pestilence, and frenzies wood,
The marrow-eating sickness whose attaint,
Disorder breeds by heating of the blood,
    Surfeits, imposthumes, grief, and damn'd despair,
    Swear nature's death, for framing thee so fair.

And not the least of all these maladies,
But in one minute's fight brings beauty under,
Both favour, savour, hue, and qualities,
Whereat th' impartial gazer late did wonder,
    Are on the sudden wasted, thaw'd, and done,
    As mountain snows melts with the midday sun.

Therefore despite of fruitless chastity,
Love-lacking vestals, and self-loving nuns,
That on the earth would breed a scarcity,
And barren dearth of daughters, and of sons;
   Be prodigal, the lamp that burns by night,
   Dries up his oil, to lend the world his light.

What is thy body but a swallowing grave,
Seeming to bury that posterity,
Which by the rights of time thou needs must have,
If thou destroy them not in dark obscurity?
   If so the world will hold thee in disdain,
   Sith in thy pride, so fair a hope is slain.

So in thyself, thyself art made away,
A mischief worse than civil home-bred strife,
Or theirs whose desperate hands themselves do slay,
Or butcher sire, that reaves his son of life:
   Foul cankering rust, the hidden treasure frets,
   But gold that's put to use more gold begets.

Nay then (quoth Adon) you will fall again,
Into your idle over-handled theme,
The kiss I gave you is bestow'd in vain,
And all in vain you strive against the stream,
   For by this black-fac'd night, desire's foul nurse,
   Your treatise makes me like you, worse and worse.

If love have lent you twenty thousand tongues,
And every tongue more moving than your own,
Bewitching like the wanton mermaid's songs,
Yet from mine ear the tempting tune is blown,
   For know my heart stands armed in mine ear,
   And will not let a false sound enter there.

Lest the deceiving harmony should run,
Into the quiet closure of my breast,
And then my little heart were quite undone,
In his bed-chamber to be barr'd of rest,
   No Lady no, my heart longs not to groan,
   But soundly sleeps, while now it sleeps alone.

What have you urg'd, that I cannot reprove?
The path is smooth that leadeth on to danger,
I hate not love, but your device in love,
That lends embracements unto every stranger,
   You do it for increase, o strange excuse!
   When reason is the bawd to lust's abuse.

Call it not love, for love to heaven is fled,
Since sweating lust on earth usurp'd his name,
Under whose simple semblance he hath fed,
Upon fresh beauty, blotting it with blame;
   Which the hot tyrant stains, and soon bereaves:
   As caterpillars do the tender leaves.

Love comforteth like sunshine after rain,
But lust's effect is tempest after sun,
Love's gentle spring doth always fresh remain,
Lust's winter comes, ere summer half be done:
   Love surfeits not, lust like a glutton dies:
   Love is all truth, lust full of forged lies.

More I could tell, but more I dare not say,
The text is old, the orator too green,
Therefore in sadness, now I will away,
My face is full of shame, my heart of teen,
   Mine ears that to your wanton talk attended,
   Do burn themselves, for having so offended.

With this he breaketh from the sweet embrace,
Of those fair arms which bound him to her breast,
And homeward through the dark lawnd runs apace,
Leaves love upon her back, deeply distress'd,
  Look how a bright star shooteth from the sky;
  So glides he in the night from Venus' eye.

Which after him she darts, as one on shore
Gazing upon a late-embarked friend,
Till the wild waves will have him seen no more,
Whose ridges with the meeting clouds contend:
  So did the merciless, and pitchy night,
  Fold in the object that did feed her sight.

Whereat amaz'd as one that unaware,
Hath dropp'd a precious jewel in the flood,
Or stonish'd, as night-wandrers often are,
Their light blown out in some mistrustful wood;
  Even so confounded in the dark she lay,
  Having lost the fair discovery of her way.

And now she beats her heart, whereat it groans,
That all the neighbour caves as seeming troubled,
Make verbal repetition of her moans,
Passion on passion, deeply is redoubled,
  Ay me, she cries, and twenty times, woe, woe,
  And twenty echoes, twenty times cry so.

She marking them, begins a wailing note,
And sings extemporally a woeful ditty,
How love makes young men thrall, and old men dote,
How love is wise in folly, foolish witty:
  Her heavy anthem still concludes in woe,
  And still the choir of echoes answer so.

Her song was tedious, and out-wore the night,
For lover's hours are long, though seeming short,
If pleas'd themselves, others they think delight,
In such like circumstance, with such like sport:
    Their copious stories oftentimes begun,
    End without audience, and are never done.

For who hath she to spend the night withal,
But idle sounds resembling parasites?
Like shrill-tongued tapsters answering every call,
Soothing the humour of fantastic wits,
    She says 'tis so, they answer all 'tis so,
    And would say after her, if she said no.

Lo here the gentle lark weary of rest,
From his moist cabinet mounts up on high,
And wakes the morning, from whose silver breast,
The sun ariseth in his majesty,
    Who doth the world so gloriously behold,
    That cedar tops and hills, seem burnish'd gold.

Venus salutes him with this fair good-morrow,
O thou clear god, and patron of all light,
From whom each lamp, and shining star doth borrow,
The beauteous influence that makes him bright,
    There lives a son that suck'd an earthly mother,
    May lend thee light, as thou dost lend to other.

This said, she hasteth to a myrtle grove,
Musing the morning is so much o'erworn,
And yet she hears no tidings of her love;
She hearkens for his hounds, and for his horn,
    Anon she hears them chant it lustily,
    And all in haste she coasteth to the cry.

And as she runs, the bushes in the way,
Some catch her by the neck, some kiss her face,
Some twin'd about her thigh to make her stay,
She wildly breaketh from their strict embrace,
  Like a milch doe, whose swelling dugs do ache,
  Hasting to feed her fawn, hid in some brake.

By this she hears the hounds are at a bay,
Whereat she starts like one that spies an adder,
Wreath'd up in fatal folds just in his way,
The fear whereof doth make him shake, and shudder,
  Even so the timorous yelping of the hounds,
  Appals her senses, and her spirit confounds.

For now she knows it is no gentle chase,
But the blunt boar, rough bear, or lion proud,
Because the cry remaineth in one place,
Where fearfully the dogs exclaim aloud,
  Finding their enemy to be so curst,
  They all strain curtsey who shall cope him first.

This dismal cry rings sadly in her ear,
Through which it enters to surprise her heart,
Who overcome by doubt, and bloodless fear,
With cold-pale weakness, numbs each feeling part,
  Like soldiers when their captain once doth yield,
  They basely fly, and dare not stay the field.

Thus stands she in a trembling ecstasy,
Till cheering up her senses all dismay'd,
She tells them 'tis a causeless fantasy,
And childish error that they are afraid,
  Bids them leave quaking, bids them fear no more,
  And with that word, she spied the hunted boar.

Whose frothy mouth, bepainted all with red,
Like milk, and blood, being mingled both together,
A second fear through all her sinews spread,
Which madly hurries her, she knows not whither,
  This way she runs, and now she will no further,
  But back retires, to rate the boar for murther.

A thousand spleens bear her a thousand ways,
She treads the path, that she untreads again;
Her more than haste, is mated with delays,
Like the proceedings of a drunken brain,
  Full of respects, yet not at all respecting,
  In hand with all things, nought at all effecting.

Here kennell'd in a brake, she finds a hound,
And asks the weary caitiff for his master,
And there another licking of his wound,
'Gainst venom'd sores, the only sovereign plaster.
  And here she meets another, sadly scowling,
  To whom she speaks, and he replies with howling.

When he hath ceas'd his ill resounding noise,
Another flapmouth'd mourner, black, and grim,
Against the welkin, volleys out his voice,
Another, and another, answer him,
  Clapping their proud tails to the ground below,
  Shaking their scratch'd ears, bleeding as they go.

Look how, the world's poor people are amazed,
At apparitions, signs, and prodigies,
Whereon with fearful eyes, they long have gazed,
Infusing them with dreadful prophecies;
  So she at these sad signs, draws up her breath,
  And sighing it again, exclaims on death.

Hard-favoured tyrant, ugly, meagre, lean,
Hateful divorce of love, (thus chides she death)
Grim-grinning ghost, earth's worm what dost thou mean?
To stifle beauty, and to steal his breath?
  Who when he liv'd, his breath and beauty set
  Gloss on the rose, smell to the violet.

If he be dead, o no, it cannot be,
Seeing his beauty, thou shouldst strike at it,
O yes, it may, thou hast no eyes to see,
But hatefully at random dost thou hit,
  Thy mark is feeble age, but thy false dart,
  Mistakes that aim, and cleaves an infant's heart.

Hadst thou but bid beware, then he had spoke,
And hearing him, thy power had lost his power,
The destinies will curse thee for this stroke,
They bid thee crop a weed, thou pluck'st a flower,
  Love's golden arrow at him should have fled,
  And not death's ebon dart to strike him dead.

Dost thou drink tears, that thou provok'st such weeping,
What may a heavy groan advantage thee?
Why hast thou cast into eternal sleeping,
Those eyes that taught all other eyes to see?
  Now nature cares not for thy mortal vigour,
  Since her best work is ruin'd with thy rigour.

Here overcome as one full of despair,
She vail'd her eye-lids, who like sluices stopp'd
The crystal tide, that from her two cheeks fair,
In the sweet channel of her bosom dropp'd.
  But through the flood-gates breaks the silver rain,
  And with his strong course opens them again.

O how her eyes, and tears, did lend, and borrow,
Her eye seen in the tears, tears in her eye,
Both crystals, where they view'd each other's sorrow;
Sorrow, that friendly sighs sought still to dry,
   But like a stormy day, now wind, now rain,
   Sighs dry her cheeks, tears make them wet again.

Variable passions throng her constant woe,
As striving who should best become her grief,
All entertain'd, each passion labours so,
That every present sorrow seemeth chief,
   But none is best, then join they all together,
   Like many clouds, consulting for foul weather.

By this far off, she hears some huntsman hallow,
A nurse's song ne'er pleased her babe so well,
The dire imagination she did follow,
This sound of hope doth labour to expel,
   For now reviving joy bids her rejoice,
   And flatters her, it is Adonis' voice.

Whereat her tears began to turn their tide,
Being prison'd in her eye: like pearls in glass,
Yet sometimes falls an orient drop beside,
Which her cheek melts, as scorning it should pass
   To wash the foul face of the sluttish ground,
   Who is but drunken when she seemeth drown'd.

O hard believing love how strange it seems!
Not to believe, and yet too credulous:
Thy weal, and woe, are both of them extremes,
Despair, and hope, makes thee ridiculous.
   The one doth flatter thee in thoughts unlikely,
   In likely thoughts the other kills thee quickly.

Now she unweaves the web that she hath wrought,
Adonis lives, and death is not to blame:
It was not she that call'd him all to nought;
Now she adds honours to his hateful name.
    She clepes him king of graves, and grave for kings,
    Imperious supreme of all mortal things.

No, no, quoth she, sweet death, I did but jest,
Yet pardon me, I felt a kind of fear
Whenas I met the boar, that bloody beast,
Which knows no pity but is still severe,
    Then gentle shadow (truth I must confess)
    I rail'd on thee, fearing my love's decease.

'Tis not my fault, the boar provok'd my tongue,
Be wreak'd on him (invisible commander)
'Tis he foul creature, that hath done thee wrong,
I did but act, he's author of thy slander.
    Grief hath two tongues, and never woman yet,
    Could rule them both, without ten women's wit.

Thus hoping that Adonis is alive,
Her rash suspect she doth extenuate,
And that his beauty may the better thrive,
With death she humbly doth insinuate.
    Tells him of trophies, statues, tombs, and stories,
    His victories, his triumphs, and his glories.

O Jove, quoth she, how much a fool was I,
To be of such a weak and silly mind,
To wail his death who lives, and must not die,
Till mutual overthrow of mortal kind?
    For he being dead, with him is beauty slain,
    And beauty dead, black Chaos comes again.

Fie, fie, fond love, thou art as full of fear,
As one with treasure laden, hemm'd with thieves,
Trifles unwitnessed with eye, or ear,
Thy coward heart with false bethinking grieves.
  Even at this word she hears a merry horn,
  Whereat she leaps, that was but late forlorn.

As falcons to the lure, away she flies,
The grass stoops not, she treads on it so light,
And in her haste, unfortunately spies,
The foul boar's conquest, on her fair delight,
  Which seen, her eyes are murdred with the view,
  Like stars asham'd of day, themselves withdrew.

Or as the snail, whose tender horns being hit,
Shrinks backward in his shelly cave with pain,
And, there all smother'd up, in shade doth sit,
Long after fearing to creep forth again:
  So at his bloody view her eyes are fled,
  Into the deep-dark cabins of her head.

Where they resign their office, and their light,
To the disposing of her troubled brain,
Who bids them still consort with ugly night,
And never wound the heart with looks again,
  Who like a king perplexed in his throne,
  By their suggestion, gives a deadly groan.

Whereat each tributary subject quakes,
As when the wind imprison'd in the ground,
Struggling for passage, earth's foundation shakes,
Which with cold terror, doth men's minds confound:
  This mutiny each part doth so surprise,
  That from their dark beds once more leap her eyes.

And being open'd, threw unwilling light,
Upon the wide wound, that the boar had trench'd
In his soft flank, whose wonted lily white
With purple tears that his wound wept, was drench'd.
   No flower was nigh, no grass, herb, leaf, or weed,
   But stole his blood, and seem'd with him to bleed.

This solemn sympathy, poor Venus noteth,
Over one shoulder doth she hang her head,
Dumbly she passions, franticly she doteth,
She thinks he could not die, he is not dead,
   Her voice is stopp'd, her joints forget to bow,
   Her eyes are mad, that they have wept till now.

Upon his hurt she looks so steadfastly,
That her sight dazzling, makes the wound seem three,
And then she reprehends her mangling eye,
That makes more gashes, where no breach should be:
   His face seems twain, each several limb is doubled,
   For oft the eye mistakes, the brain being troubled.

My tongue cannot express my grief for one,
And yet (quoth she) behold two Adons dead,
My sighs are blown away, my salt tears gone,
Mine eyes are turn'd to fire, my heart to lead,
   Heavy heart's lead melt at mine eyes' red fire,
   So shall I die by drops of hot desire.

Alas poor world what treasure hast thou lost,
What face remains alive that's worth the viewing?
Whose tongue is music now? what canst thou boast,
Of things long since, or any thing ensuing?
   The flowers are sweet, their colours fresh, and trim,
   But true sweet beauty liv'd, and died with him.

Bonnet, nor veil henceforth no creature wear,
Nor sun, nor wind will ever strive to kiss you,
Having no fair to lose, you need not fear,
The sun doth scorn you, and the wind doth hiss you.
  But when Adonis liv'd, sun, and sharp air,
  Lurk'd like two thieves, to rob him of his fair.

And therefore would he put his bonnet on,
Under whose brim the gaudy sun would peep,
The wind would blow it off, and being gone,
Play with his locks, then would Adonis weep.
  And straight in pity of his tender years,
  They both would strive who first should dry his tears.

To see his face the Lion walk'd along,
Behind some hedge, because he would not fear him:
To recreate himself when he hath song,
The Tiger would be tame, and gently hear him.
  If he had spoke, the wolf would leave his prey,
  And never fright the silly lamb that day.

When he beheld his shadow in the brook,
The fishes spread on it their golden gills,
When he was by the birds such pleasure took,
That some would sing, some others in their bills
  Would bring him mulberries and ripe-red cherries,
  He fed them with his sight, they him with berries.

But this foul, grim, and urchin-snouted boar,
Whose downward eye still looketh for a grave:
Ne'er saw the beauteous livery that he wore,
Witness the entertainment that he gave.
  If he did see his face, why then I know,
  He thought to kiss him, and hath kill'd him so.

'Tis true, 'tis true, thus was Adonis slain,
He ran upon the boar with his sharp spear,
Who did not whet his teeth at him again,
But by a kiss thought to persuade him there.
   And nousling in his flank the loving swine,
   Sheath'd unaware the tusk in his soft groin.

Had I been tooth'd like him I must confess,
With kissing him I should have kill'd him first,
But he is dead, and never did he bless
My youth with his, the more am I accurst.
   With this she falleth in the place she stood,
   And stains her face with his congealed blood.

She looks upon his lips, and they are pale,
She takes him by the hand, and that is cold,
She whispers in his ears a heavy tale,
As if they heard the woeful words she told;
   She lifts the coffer-lids that close his eyes,
   Where lo, two lamps burnt out in darkness lies.

Two glasses where herself, herself beheld
A thousand times, and now no more reflect,
Their virtue lost, wherein they late excell'd,
And every beauty robb'd of his effect;
   Wonder of time (quoth she) this is my spite,
   That thou being dead, the day should yet be light.

Since thou art dead, lo here I prophesy,
Sorrow on love hereafter shall attend:
It shall be waited on with jealousy,
Find sweet beginning, but unsavoury end.
   Ne'er settled equally, but high or low,
   That all love's pleasure shall not match his woe.

It shall be fickle, false, and full of fraud,
Bud, and be blasted, in a breathing while,
The bottom poison, and the top o'er-straw'd
With sweets, that shall the truest sight beguile,
  The strongest body shall it make most weak,
  Strike the wise dumb, and teach the fool to speak.

It shall be sparing, and too full of riot,
Teaching decrepit age to tread the measures,
The staring ruffian shall it keep in quiet,
Pluck down the rich, enrich the poor with treasures,
  It shall be raging mad, and silly mild,
  Make the young old, the old become a child.

It shall suspect where is no cause of fear,
It shall not fear where it should most mistrust,
It shall be merciful, and too severe,
And most deceiving, when it seems most just,
  Perverse it shall be, where it shows most toward,
  Put fear to valour, courage to the coward.

It shall be cause of war, and dire events,
And set dissension 'twixt the son, and sire,
Subject, and servile to all discontents:
As dry combustious matter is to fire,
  Sith in his prime, death doth my love destroy,
  They that love best, their loves shall not enjoy.

By this the boy that by her side lay kill'd,
Was melted like a vapour from her sight,
And in his blood that on the ground lay spill'd,
A purple flower sprung up, chequer'd with white,
  Resembling well his pale cheeks, and the blood,
  Which in round drops, upon their whiteness stood.

She bows her head, the new-sprung flower to smell,
Comparing it to her Adonis' breath,
And says within her bosom it shall dwell,
Since he himself is reft from her by death;
*   She crops the stalk, and in the breach appears,*
*   Green-dropping sap, which she compares to tears.*

Poor flower (quoth she) this was thy father's guise,
Sweet issue of a more sweet smelling sire,
For every little grief to wet his eyes,
To grow unto himself was his desire;
*   And so 'tis thine, but know it is as good,*
*   To wither in my breast, as in his blood.*

Here was thy father's bed, here in my breast,
Thou art the next of blood, and 'tis thy right.
Lo in this hollow cradle take thy rest,
My throbbing heart shall rock thee day and night;
*   There shall not be one minute in an hour,*
*   Wherein I will not kiss my sweet love's flower.*

Thus weary of the world, away she hies,
And yokes her silver doves, by whose swift aid,
Their mistress mounted through the empty skies,
In her light chariot, quickly is convey'd,
*   Holding their course to Paphos, where their queen*
*   Means to immure herself, and not be seen.*

FINIS

The Rape of Lucrece

To the Right Honourable

HENRY WRIOTHESLEY

Earl of Southampton, and
Baron of Titchfield

THE love I dedicate to your Lordship is without end: whereof this Pamphlet without beginning is but a superfluous moiety. The warrant I have of your Honourable disposition, not the worth of my untutor'd lines makes it assured of acceptance. What I have done is yours, what I have to do is yours, being part in all I have, devoted yours. Were my worth greater, my duty would show greater, mean time, as it is, it is bound to your Lordship; To whom I wish long life still lengthened with all happiness.

Your Lordships in all duty,

WILLIAM SHAKESPEARE

THE ARGUMENT

LUCIUS TARQUINIUS (*for his excessive pride surnamed Superbus*) *after he had caused his own father-in-law Servius Tullius to be cruelly murdred, and contrary to the Roman laws and customs, not requiring or staying for the people's suffrages, had possessed himself of the kingdom: went accompanied with his sons and other Noblemen of Rome, to besiege Ardea, during which siege, the principal men of the Army meeting one evening at the tent of Sextus Tarquinius, the King's son, in their discourses after supper every one commended the virtues of his own wife: among whom Colatinus extolled the incomparable chastity of his wife Lucretia. In that pleasant humour they all posted to Rome, and intending by their secret and sudden arrival to make trial of that which every one had before avouched, only Colatinus finds his wife (though it were late in the night) spinning amongst her maids, the other Ladies were all found dancing and revelling, or in several disports: whereupon the Noblemen yielded Colatinus the victory, and his wife the fame. At that time Sextus Tarquinius being enflamed with Lucrece' beauty, yet smothering his passions for the present, departed with the rest back to the camp: from whence he shortly after privily withdrew himself, and was (according to his estate) royally entertained and lodged by Lucrece at Colatium. The same night he treacherously stealeth into her chamber, violently ravish'd her, and early in the morning speedeth away. Lucrece in this lamentable plight, hastily dispatcheth messengers, one to Rome for her father, another to the Camp for Colatine. They came, the one accompanied with Junius Brutus, the other with Publius Valerius: and finding Lucrece attired in mourning habit, demanded the cause of her sorrow. She first taking an oath of them for her revenge, revealed the actor, and whole manner of his dealing, and withal suddenly stabbed herself. Which done, with one consent they all vowed to root out the whole hated family of the Tarquins: and bearing the dead body to Rome, Brutus acquainted the people with the doer and manner of the vile deed: with a bitter invective against the tyranny of the King, wherewith the people were so moved, that with one consent and a general acclamation, the Tarquins were all exiled, and the state government changed from Kings to Consuls.*

THE RAPE OF LUCRECE

From the besieged Ardea all in post,
Borne by the trustless wings of false desire,
Lust-breathed Tarquin, leaves the Roman host,
And to Colatium bears the lightless fire,
Which in pale embers hid, lurks to aspire,
    And girdle with embracing flames, the waist
    Of Colatine's fair love, Lucrece the chaste.

Hap'ly that name of chaste, unhapp'ly set
This bateless edge on his keen appetite:
When Colatine unwisely did not let,
To praise the clear unmatched red and white,
Which triumph'd in that sky of his delight:
    Where mortal stars as bright as heaven's Beauties,
    With pure aspects did him peculiar duties.

For he the night before in Tarquin's tent,
Unlock'd the treasure of his happy state:
What priceless wealth the heavens had him lent,
In the possession of his beauteous mate.
Reckning his fortune at such high proud rate,
    That Kings might be espoused to more fame,
    But King nor Peer to such a peerless dame.

O happiness enjoy'd but of a few,
And, if possess'd as soon decay'd and done:
As is the morning's silver melting dew,
Against the golden splendour of the Sun,
An expir'd date cancell'd ere well begun.
    Honour and Beauty in the owner's arms,
    Are weakly fortress'd from a world of harms.

Beauty itself doth of itself persuade,
The eyes of men without an orator,
What needeth then apology be made
To set forth that which is so singular?
Or why is Colatine the publisher
      Of that rich jewel he should keep unknown,
      From thievish ears because it is his own?

Perchance his boast of Lucrece' sovereignty,
Suggested this proud issue of a King:
For by our ears our hearts oft tainted be:
Perchance that envy of so rich a thing
Braving compare, disdainfully did sting
      His high pitch'd thoughts that meaner men should vaunt,
      That golden hap which their superiors want.

But some untimely thought did instigate,
His all too timeless speed if none of those,
His honour, his affairs, his friends, his state,
Neglected all, with swift intent he goes,
To quench the coal which in his liver glows.
      O rash false heat, wrapp'd in repentant cold,
      Thy hasty spring still blasts and ne'er grows old.

When at Colatium this false Lord arrived,
Well was he welcom'd by the Roman dame,
Within whose face Beauty and Virtue strived,
Which of them both should underprop her fame.
When Virtue bragg'd, Beauty would blush for shame,
      When Beauty boasted blushes, in despite
      Virtue would stain that o'er with silver white.

But Beauty in that white entituled,
From Venus' doves doth challenge that fair field,
Then Virtue claims from Beauty, Beauty's red,
Which Virtue gave the golden age, to gild
Their silver cheeks, and call'd it then their shield,
　　Teaching them thus to use it in the fight,
　　When shame assail'd, the red should fence the white.

This Heraldry in Lucrece' face was seen,
Argued by Beauty's red and Virtue's white,
Of either's colour was the other Queen:
Proving from world's minority their right,
Yet their ambition makes them still to fight:
　　The sovereignty of either being so great,
　　That oft they interchange each other's seat.

This silent war of lilies and of roses,
Which Tarquin view'd in her fair face's field,
In their pure ranks his traitor eye encloses,
Where lest between them both it should be kill'd,
The coward captive vanquished, doth yield
　　To those two armies that would let him go,
　　Rather than triumph in so false a foe.

Now thinks he that her husband's shallow tongue,
The niggard prodigal that prais'd her so:
In that high task hath done her Beauty wrong,
Which far exceeds his barren skill to show.
Therefore that praise which Colatine doth owe,
　　Enchanted Tarquin answers with surmise,
　　In silent wonder of still gazing eyes.

This earthly saint adored by this devil,
Little suspecteth the false worshipper:
"For unstain'd thoughts do seldom dream on evil.
"Birds never lim'd, no secret bushes fear:
So guiltless she securely gives good cheer,
    And reverend welcome to her princely guest,
    Whose inward ill no outward harm express'd.

For that he colour'd with his high estate,
Hiding base sin in pleats of Majesty;
That nothing in him seem'd inordinate,
Save sometime too much wonder of his eye,
Which having all, all could not satisfy;
    But poorly rich so wanteth in his store,
    That cloy'd with much, he pineth still for more.

But she that never cop'd with stranger eyes,
Could pick no meaning from their parling looks,
Nor read the subtle shining secrecies,
Writ in the glassy margents of such books,
She touch'd no unknown baits, nor fear'd no hooks,
    Nor could she moralize his wanton sight,
    More than his eyes were open'd to the light.

He stories to her ears her husband's fame,
Won in the fields of fruitful Italy:
And decks with praises Colatine's high name,
Made glorious by his manly chivalry,
With bruised arms and wreaths of victory,
    Her joy with heav'd-up hand she doth express,
    And wordless so greets heaven for his success.

Far from the purpose of his coming thither,
He makes excuses for his being there,
No cloudy show of stormy blustring weather,
Doth yet in his fair welkin once appear,
Till sable Night mother of dread and fear,
   Upon the world dim darkness doth display,
   And in her vaulty prison, stows the day.

For then is Tarquin brought unto his bed,
Intending weariness with heavy spright:
For after supper long he questioned,
With modest Lucrece, and wore out the night,
Now leaden slumber with life's strength doth fight,
   And every one to rest himself betakes,
   Save thieves, and cares, and troubled minds that wakes.

As one of which doth Tarquin lie revolving
The sundry dangers of his will's obtaining:
Yet ever to obtain his will resolving,
Though weak built hopes persuade him to abstaining:
Despair to gain doth traffic oft for gaining,
   And when great treasure is the meed proposed,
   Though death be adjunct, there's no death supposed.

Those that much covet are with gain so fond,
That what they have not, that which they possess
They scatter and unloose it from their bond,
And so by hoping more they have but less,
Or gaining more, the profit of excess
   Is but to surfeit, and such griefs sustain,
   That they prove bankrout in this poor rich gain.

The aim of all is but to nurse the life,
With honour, wealth, and ease, in waning age:
And in this aim there is such thwarting strife,
That one for all, or all for one we gage:
As life for honour, in fell battle's rage,
 Honour for wealth, and oft that wealth doth cost
 The death of all, and altogether lost.

So that in ventring ill, we leave to be
The things we are, for that which we expect:
And this ambitious foul infirmity,
In having much torments us with defect
Of that we have: so then we do neglect
 The thing we have, and all for want of wit,
 Make something nothing, by augmenting it.

Such hazard now must doting Tarquin make,
Pawning his honour to obtain his lust,
And for himself, himself he must forsake.
Then where is truth if there be no self-trust?
When shall he think to find a stranger just,
 When he himself, himself confounds, betrays,
 To slandrous tongues and wretched hateful days?

Now stole upon the time the dead of night,
When heavy sleep had clos'd up mortal eyes,
No comfortable star did lend his light,
No noise but owls, and wolves' death-boding cries:
Now serves the season that they may surprise
 The silly lambs, pure thoughts are dead and still,
 While Lust and Murder wakes to stain and kill.

And now this lustful Lord leapt from his bed,
Throwing his mantle rudely o'er his arm,
Is madly toss'd between desire and dread;
Th' one sweetly flatters, th' other feareth harm,
But honest fear, bewitch'd with lust's foul charm,
   Doth too too oft betake him to retire,
   Beaten away by brainsick rude desire.

His falchion on a flint he softly smiteth,
That from the cold stone sparks of fire do fly,
Whereat a waxen torch forthwith he lighteth,
Which must be lodestar to his lustful eye.
And to the flame thus speaks advisedly;
   As from this cold flint I enforc'd this fire,
   So Lucrece must I force to my desire.

Here pale with fear he doth premeditate,
The dangers of his loathsome enterprise:
And in his inward mind he doth debate,
What following sorrow may on this arise.
Then looking scornfully, he doth despise
   His naked armour of still slaughter'd lust,
   And justly thus controls his thoughts unjust.

Fair torch burn out thy light, and lend it not
To darken her whose light excelleth thine:
And die unhallow'd thoughts, before you blot
With your uncleanness, that which is divine:
Offer pure incense to so pure a shrine:
   Let fair humanity abhor the deed,
   That spots and stains love's modest snow-white weed.

O shame to knighthood, and to shining arms,
O foul dishonour to my household's grave:
O impious act including all foul harms.
A martial man to be soft fancy's slave,
True valour still a true respect should have,
    Then my digression is so vile, so base,
    That it will live engraven in my face.

Yea though I die the scandal will survive,
And be an eye-sore in my golden coat:
Some loathsome dash the Herald will contrive,
To cipher me how fondly I did dote:
That my posterity sham'd with the note
    Shall curse my bones, and hold it for no sin,
    To wish that I their father had not been.

What win I if I gain the thing I seek?
A dream, a breath, a froth of fleeting joy.
Who buys a minute's mirth to wail a week?
Or sells eternity to get a toy?
For one sweet grape who will the vine destroy?
    Or what fond beggar, but to touch the crown,
    Would with the sceptre straight be stroken down?

If Colatinus dream of my intent,
Will he not wake, and in a desp'rate rage
Post hither, this vile purpose to prevent?
This siege that hath engirt his marriage,
This blur to youth, this sorrow to the sage,
    This dying virtue, this surviving shame,
    Whose crime will bear an ever-during blame.

O what excuse can my invention make
When thou shalt charge me with so black a deed?
Will not my tongue be mute, my frail joints shake?
Mine eyes forgo their light, my false heart bleed?
The guilt being great, the fear doth still exceed;
  And extreme fear can neither fight not fly,
  But cowardlike with trembling terror die.

Had Colatinus kill'd my son or sire,
Or lain in ambush to betray my life,
Or were he not my dear friend, this desire
Might have excuse to work upon his wife:
As in revenge or quittal of such strife.
  But as he is my kinsman, my dear friend,
  The shame and faults finds no excuse nor end.

Shameful it is: ay, if the fact be known,
Hateful it is: there is no hate in loving,
I'll beg her love: but she is not her own:
The worst is but denial and reproving.
My will is strong past reason's weak removing:
  Who fears a sentence or an old man's saw,
  Shall by a painted cloth be kept in awe.

Thus graceless holds he disputation,
'Tween frozen conscience and hot-burning will,
And with good thoughts makes dispensation,
Urging the worser sense for vantage still.
Which in a moment doth confound and kill
  All pure effects, and doth so far proceed,
  That what is vile, shows like a virtuous deed.

Quoth he, she took me kindly by the hand,
And gaz'd for tidings in my eager eyes,
Fearing some hard news from the warlike band,
Where her beloved Colatinus lies.
O how her fear did make her colour rise!
   First red as roses that on lawn we lay,
   Then white as lawn the roses took away.

And how her hand in my hand being lock'd,
Forc'd it to tremble with her loyal fear:
Which struck her sad, and then it faster rock'd,
Until her husband's welfare she did hear.
Whereat she smiled with so sweet a cheer,
   That had Narcissus seen her as she stood,
   Self-love had never drown'd him in the flood.

Why hunt I then for colour or excuses?
All orators are dumb when Beauty pleadeth,
Poor wretches have remorse in poor abuses,
Love thrives not in the heart that shadows dreadeth,
Affection is my Captain, and he leadeth.
   And when his gaudy banner is display'd,
   The coward fights, and will not be dismay'd.

Then childish fear avaunt, debating die,
Respect and reason wait on wrinkled age:
My heart shall never countermand mine eye:
Sad pause, and deep regard beseems the sage,
My part is youth and beats these from the stage.
   Desire my Pilot is, Beauty my prize,
   Then who fears sinking where such treasure lies?

As corn o'ergrown by weeds: so heedful fear
Is almost choked by unresisted lust:
Away he steals with open listning ear,
Full of foul hope, and full of fond mistrust:
Both which as servitors to the unjust,
  So cross him with their opposite persuasion,
  That now he vows a league, and now invasion.

Within his thought her heavenly image sits,
And in the selfsame seat sits Colatine,
That eye which looks on her confounds his wits,
That eye which him beholds, as more divine,
Unto a view so false will not incline;
  But with a pure appeal seeks to the heart,
  Which once corrupted takes the worser part.

And therein heartens up his servile powers,
Who flatter'd by their leader's jocund show,
Stuff up his lust: as minutes fill up hours.
And as their Captain: so their pride doth grow,
Paying more slavish tribute than they owe.
  By reprobate desire thus madly led,
  The Roman Lord marcheth to Lucrece' bed.

The locks between her chamber and his will,
Each one by him enforc'd retires his ward:
But as they open they all rate his ill,
Which drives the creeping thief to some regard,
The threshold grates the door to have him heard,
  Night-wandring weasels shriek to see him there,
  They fright him, yet he still pursues his fear.

As each unwilling portal yields him way,
Through little vents and crannies of the place,
The wind wars with his torch, to make him stay,
And blows the smoke of it into his face,
Extinguishing his conduct in this case.
    But his hot heart, which fond desire doth scorch,
    Puffs forth another wind that fires the torch.

And being lighted, by the light he spies
Lucretia's glove, wherein her needle sticks,
He takes it from the rushes where it lies,
And griping it, the needle his finger pricks.
As who should say, this glove to wanton tricks
    Is not inur'd; return again in haste,
    Thou see'st our mistress' ornaments are chaste.

But all these poor forbiddings could not stay him,
He in the worst sense consters their denial:
The doors, the wind, the glove, that did delay him,
He takes for accidental things of trial.
Or as those bars which stop the hourly dial,
    Who with a lingering stay his course doth let,
    Till every minute pays the hour his debt.

So so, quoth he, these lets attend the time,
Like little frosts that sometime threat the spring,
To add a more rejoicing to the prime,
And give the sneaped birds more cause to sing.
Pain pays the income of each precious thing,
    Huge rocks, high winds, strong pirates, shelves and sands
    The merchant fears, ere rich at home he lands.

Now is he come unto the chamber door,
That shuts him from the Heaven of his thought,
Which with a yielding latch, and with no more,
Hath barr'd him from the blessed thing he sought.
So from himself impiety hath wrought,
    That for his prey to pray he doth begin,
    As if the Heavens should countenance his sin.

But in the midst of his unfruitful prayer,
Having solicited th' eternal power,
That his foul thoughts might compass his fair fair,
And they would stand auspicious to the hour.
Even there he starts, quoth he, I must deflower;
    The powers to whom I pray abhor this fact,
    How can they then assist me in the act?

Then Love and Fortune be my Gods, my guide,
My will is back'd with resolution:
Thoughts are but dreams till their effects be tried,
The blackest sin is clear'd with absolution.
Against love's fire, fear's frost hath dissolution.
    The eye of Heaven is out, and misty night
    Covers the shame that follows sweet delight.

This said, his guilty hand pluck'd up the latch,
And with his knee the door he opens wide,
The dove sleeps fast that this night owl will catch.
Thus treason works ere traitors be espied.
Who sees the lurking serpent steps aside;
    But she sound sleeping fearing no such thing,
    Lies at the mercy of his mortal sting.

Into the chamber wickedly he stalks,
And gazeth on her yet unstained bed:
The curtains being close, about he walks,
Rolling his greedy eyeballs in his head.
By their high treason is his heart misled,
    Which gives the watch-word to his hand full soon,
    To draw the cloud that hides the silver Moon.

Look as the fair and fiery pointed Sun,
Rushing from forth a cloud, bereaves our sight:
Even so the curtain drawn, his eyes begun
To wink, being blinded with a greater light.
Whether it is that she reflects so bright,
    That dazzleth them, or else some shame supposed,
    But blind they are, and keep themselves enclosed.

O had they in that darksome prison died,
Then had they seen the period of their ill:
Then Colatine again by Lucrece' side,
In his clear bed might have reposed still.
But they must ope this blessed league to kill,
    And holy-thoughted Lucrece to their sight,
    Must sell her joy, her life, her world's delight.

Her lily hand, her rosy cheek lies under,
Cozening the pillow of a lawful kiss:
Who therefore angry seems to part in sunder,
Swelling on either side to want his bliss.
Between whose hills her head entombed is;
    Where like a virtuous monument she lies,
    To be admir'd of lewd unhallow'd eyes.

Without the bed her other fair hand was,
On the green coverlet whose perfect white
Show'd like an April daisy on the grass,
With pearly sweat resembling dew of night.
Her eyes like marigolds had sheath'd their light,
   And canopied in darkness sweetly lay,
   Till they might open to adorn the day.

Her hair like golden threads play'd with her breath,
O modest wantons, wanton modesty!
Showing life's triumph in the map of death,
And death's dim look in life's mortality.
Each in her sleep themselves so beautify,
   As if between them twain there were no strife,
   But that life liv'd in death, and death in life.

Her breasts like ivory globes circled with blue,
A pair of maiden worlds unconquered,
Save of their Lord, no bearing yoke they knew,
And him by oath they truly honoured.
These worlds in Tarquin new ambition bred,
   Who like a foul usurper went about,
   From this fair throne to heave the owner out.

What could he see but mightily he noted?
What did he note, but strongly he desired?
What he beheld, on that he firmly doted,
And in his will his wilful eye he tired.
With more than admiration he admired
   Her azure veins, her alablaster skin,
   Her coral lips, her snow-white dimpled chin.

As the grim Lion fawneth o'er his prey,
Sharp hunger by the conquest satisfied:
So o'er this sleeping soul doth Tarquin stay,
His rage of lust by gazing qualified;
Slack'd, not suppress'd, for standing by her side,
    His eye, which late this mutiny restrains,
    Unto a greater uproar tempts his veins.

And they like straggling slaves for pillage fighting,
Obdurate vassals fell exploits effecting,
In bloody death and ravishment delighting;
Nor children's tears nor mothers' groans respecting,
Swell in their pride, the onset still expecting:
    Anon his beating heart alarum striking,
    Gives the hot charge, and bids them do their liking.

His drumming heart cheers up his burning eye,
His eye commends the leading to his hand;
His hand as proud of such a dignity,
Smoking with pride, march'd on, to make his stand
On her bare breast, the heart of all her land;
    Whose ranks of blue veins as his hand did scale,
    Left their round turrets destitute and pale.

They mustring to the quiet cabinet,
Where their dear governess and lady lies,
Do tell her she is dreadfully beset,
And fright her with confusion of their cries.
She much amaz'd breaks ope her lock'd up eyes,
    Who peeping forth this tumult to behold,
    Are by his flaming torch dimm'd and controll'd.

Imagine her as one in dead of night,
From forth dull sleep by dreadful fancy waking,
That thinks she hath beheld some ghastly sprite,
Whose grim aspect sets every joint a-shaking,
What terror 'tis: but she in worser taking,
  From sleep disturbed, heedfully doth view
  The sight which makes supposed terror true.

Wrapp'd and confounded in a thousand fears,
Like to a new-kill'd bird she trembling lies:
She dares not look, yet winking there appears
Quick-shifting antics ugly in her eyes.
"Such shadows are the weak brain's forgeries,
  Who angry that the eyes fly from their lights,
  In darkness daunts them with more dreadful sights.

His hand that yet remains upon her breast,
(Rude ram to batter such an ivory wall):
May feel her heart (poor citizen) distress'd,
Wounding itself to death, rise up and fall;
Beating her bulk, that his hand shakes withal.
  This moves in him more rage and lesser pity,
  To make the breach and enter this sweet city.

First like a trumpet doth his tongue begin,
To sound a parley to his heartless foe,
Who o'er the white sheet peers her whiter chin,
The reason of this rash alarm to know,
Which he by dumb demeanour seeks to show.
  But she with vehement prayers urgeth still,
  Under what colour he commits this ill.

Thus he replies, the colour in thy face,
That even for anger makes the lily pale,
And the red rose blush at her own disgrace,
Shall plead for me and tell my loving tale.
Under that colour am I come to scale
   Thy never-conquer'd fort, the fault is thine,
   For those thine eyes betray thee unto mine.

Thus I forestall thee, if thou mean to chide,
Thy beauty hath ensnar'd thee to this night,
Where thou with patience must my will abide,
My will that marks thee for my earth's delight,
Which I to conquer sought with all my might.
   But as reproof and reason beat it dead,
   By thy bright beauty was it newly bred.

I see what crosses my attempt will bring,
I know what thorns the growing rose defends,
I think the honey guarded with a sting,
All this before-hand counsel comprehends.
But Will is deaf, and hears no heedful friends,
   Only he hath an eye to gaze on Beauty,
   And dotes on what he looks, 'gainst law or duty.

I have debated even in my soul,
What wrong, what shame, what sorrow I shall breed,
But nothing can affection's course control,
Or stop the headlong fury of his speed.
I know repentant tears ensue the deed,
   Reproach, disdain, and deadly enmity,
   Yet strive I to embrace mine infamy.

This said, he shakes aloft his Roman blade,
Which like a falcon tow'ring in the skies,
Coucheth the fowl below with his wings' shade,
Whose crooked beak threats, if he mount he dies.
So under his insulting falchion lies
    Harmless Lucretia marking what he tells,
    With trembling fear: as fowl hear falcon's bells.

Lucrece, quoth he, this night I must enjoy thee,
If thou deny, then force must work my way:
For in thy bed I purpose to destroy thee.
That done, some worthless slave of thine I'll slay.
To kill thine honour with thy life's decay.
    And in thy dead arms do I mean to place him,
    Swearing I slew him seeing thee embrace him.

So thy surviving husband shall remain
The scornful mark of every open eye,
Thy kinsmen hang their heads at this disdain,
Thy issue blurr'd with nameless bastardy;
And thou the author of their obloquy,
    Shalt have thy trespass cited up in rhymes,
    And sung by children in succeeding times.

But if thou yield, I rest thy secret friend,
The fault unknown, is as a thought unacted,
"A little harm done to a great good end,
For lawful policy remains enacted.
"The poisonous simple sometime is compacted
    In a pure compound; being so applied,
    His venom in effect is purified.

Then for thy husband and thy children's sake,
Tender my suit, bequeath not to their lot
The shame that from them no device can take,
The blemish that will never be forgot:
Worse than a slavish wipe, or birth-hour's blot,
  For marks descried in men's nativity,
  Are nature's faults, not their own infamy.

Here with a cockatrice' dead killing eye,
He rouseth up himself, and makes a pause,
While she the picture of pure piety,
Like a white hind under the gripe's sharp claws,
Pleads in a wilderness where are no laws,
  To the rough beast, that knows no gentle right,
  Nor aught obeys but his foul appetite.

But when a black-faced cloud the world doth threat,
In his dim mist th' aspiring mountains hiding:
From earth's dark womb, some gentle gust doth get,
Which blows these pitchy vapours from their biding:
Hindring their present fall by this dividing.
  So his unhallow'd haste her words delays,
  And moody Pluto winks while Orpheus plays.

Yet foul night-waking cat he doth but dally,
While in his hold-fast foot the weak mouse panteth,
Her sad behaviour feeds his vulture folly,
A swallowing gulf that even in plenty wanteth.
His ear her prayers admits, but his heart granteth
  No penetrable entrance to her plaining,
  "Tears harden lust, though marble wear with raining.

Her pity-pleading eyes are sadly fixed
In the remorseless wrinkles of his face.
Her modest eloquence with sighs is mixed,
Which to her oratory adds more grace.
She puts the period often from his place,
  And midst the sentence so her accent breaks,
  That twice she doth begin ere once she speaks.

She conjures him by high Almighty Jove,
By knighthood, gentry, and sweet friendship's oath,
By her untimely tears, her husband's love,
By holy humane law, and common troth,
By Heaven and Earth, and all the power of both:
  That to his borrow'd bed he make retire,
  And stoop to Honour, not to foul desire.

Quoth she, reward not hospitality,
With such black payment, as thou hast pretended,
Mud not the fountain that gave drink to thee,
Mar not the thing that cannot be amended.
End thy ill aim, before thy shoot be ended.
  He is no wood-man that doth bend his bow,
  To strike a poor unseasonable doe.

My husband is thy friend, for his sake spare me,
Thyself art mighty, for thine own sake leave me:
Myself a weakling, do not then ensnare me.
Thou look'st not like deceit, do not deceive me.
My sighs like whirlwinds labour hence to heave thee.
  If ever man were mov'd with woman's moans,
  Be moved with my tears, my sighs, my groans.

All which together like a troubled Ocean,
Beat at thy rocky, and wrack-threat'ning heart,
To soften it with their continual motion:
For stones dissolv'd to water do convert.
O if no harder than a stone thou art,
   Melt at my tears and be compassionate,
   Soft pity enters at an iron gate.

In Tarquin's likeness I did entertain thee,
Hast thou put on his shape, to do him shame?
To all the Host of Heaven I complain me.
Thou wrong'st his honour, wound'st his princely name:
Thou art not what thou seem'st, and if the same,
   Thou seem'st not what thou art, a God, a King;
   For kings like Gods should govern every thing.

How will thy shame be seeded in thine age
When thus thy vices bud before thy spring?
If in thy hope thou dar'st do such outrage,
What dar'st thou not when once thou art a King?
O be remembred, no outrageous thing
   From vassal actors can be wip'd away,
   Then Kings' midseeds cannot be hid in clay.

This deed will make thee only lov'd for fear,
But happy Monarchs still are fear'd for love:
With foul offenders thou perforce must bear,
When they in thee the like offences prove;
If but for fear of this, thy will remove.
   For Princes are the glass, the school, the book,
   Where subjects' eyes do learn, do read, do look.

And wilt thou be the school where lust shall learn?
Must he in thee read lectures of such shame?
Wilt thou be glass wherein it shall discern
Authority for sin, warrant for blame?
To privilege dishonour in thy name.
  Thou back'st reproach against long-living laud,
  And mak'st fair reputation but a bawd.

Hast thou command? by him that gave it thee
From a pure heart command thy rebel will:
Draw not thy sword to guard iniquity,
For it was lent thee all that brood to kill.
Thy princely office how canst thou fulfil?
  When pattern'd by thy fault foul sin may say,
  He learn'd to sin, and thou didst teach the way.

Think but how vile a spectacle it were,
To view thy present trespass in another:
Men's faults do seldom to themselves appear,
Their own transgressions partially they smother,
This guilt would seem death-worthy in thy brother.
  O how are they wrapp'd in with infamies,
  That from their own misdeeds askance their eyes?

To thee, to thee, my heav'd up hands appeal,
Not to seducing lust thy rash relier:
I sue for exil'd majesty's repeal,
Let him return, and flattring thoughts retire.
His true respect will prison false desire,
  And wipe the dim mist from thy doting eyne,
  That thou shalt see thy state, and pity mine.

Have done, quoth he, my uncontrolled tide
Turns not, but swells the higher by this let.
Small lights are soon blown out, huge fires abide,
And with the wind in greater fury fret :
The petty streams that pay a daily debt
  To their salt sovereign with their fresh falls' haste,
  Add to his flow, but alter not his taste.

Thou art, quoth she, a sea, a sovereign King,
And lo there falls into thy boundless flood,
Black lust, dishonour, shame, mis-governing,
Who seek to stain the Ocean of thy blood.
If all these petty ills shall change thy good,
  Thy sea within a puddle's womb is hearsed,
  And not the puddle in thy sea dispersed.

So shall these slaves be King, and thou their slave,
Thou nobly base, they basely dignified :
Thou their fair life, and they thy fouler grave :
Thou loathed in their shame, they in thy pride,
The lesser thing should not the greater hide.
  The cedar stoops not to the base shrub's foot,
  But low shrubs wither at the cedar's root.

So let thy thoughts low vassals to thy state,
No more, quoth he, by Heaven I will not hear thee.
Yield to my love, if not enforced hate,
Instead of love's coy touch shall rudely tear thee.
That done, despitefully I mean to bear thee
  Unto the base bed of some rascal groom,
  To be thy partner in this shameful doom.

This said, he sets his foot upon the light,
For light and lust are deadly enemies,
Shame folded up in blind concealing night,
When most unseen, then most doth tyrannize.
The wolf hath seiz'd his prey, the poor lamb cries,
   Till with her own white fleece her voice controll'd,
   Entombs her outcry in her lips' sweet fold.

For with the nightly linen that she wears,
He pens her piteous clamours in her head,
Cooling his hot face in the chastest tears,
That ever modest eyes with sorrow shed.
O that prone lust should stain so pure a bed,
   The spots whereof could weeping purify,
   Her tears should drop on them perpetually.

But she hath lost a dearer thing than life,
And he hath won what he would lose again,
This forced league doth force a further strife,
This momentary joy breeds months of pain,
This hot desire converts to cold disdain;
   Pure chastity is rifled of her store,
   And lust the thief far poorer than before.

Look as the full-fed hound, or gorged hawk,
Unapt for tender smell, or speedy flight,
Make slow pursuit, or altogether balk,
The prey wherein by nature they delight:
So surfeit-taking Tarquin fares this night:
   His taste delicious, in digestion souring,
   Devours his will that liv'd by foul devouring.

O deeper sin than bottomless conceit
Can comprehend in still imagination!
Drunken Desire must vomit his receipt
Ere he can see his own abomination.
While Lust is in his pride no exclamation
   Can curb his heat, or rein his rash desire,
    Till like a jade, self-will himself doth tire.

And then with lank, and lean discolour'd cheek,
With heavy eye, knit-brow, and strengthless pace,
Feeble desire all recreant, poor and meek,
Like to a bankrout beggar wails his case:
The flesh being proud, Desire doth fight with grace;
   For there it revels, and when that decays,
    The guilty rebel for remission prays.

So fares it with this fault-full Lord of Rome,
Who this accomplishment so hotly chased,
For now against himself he sounds this doom,
That through the length of times he stands disgraced:
Besides his soul's fair temple is defaced,
   To whose weak ruins muster troops of cares,
    To ask the spotted Princess how she fares.

She says her subjects with foul insurrection,
Have batter'd down her consecrated wall,
And by their mortal fault brought in subjection
Her immortality, and made her thrall,
To living death and pain perpetual.
   Which in her prescience she controlled still,
    But her foresight could not forestall their will.

Ev'n in this thought through the dark night he stealeth,
A captive victor that hath lost in gain,
Bearing away the wound that nothing healeth,
The scar that will despite of cure remain,
Leaving his spoil perplex'd in greater pain.
 She bears the load of lust he left behind,
 And he the burthen of a guilty mind.

He like a thievish dog creeps sadly thence,
She like a wearied lamb lies panting there,
He scowls and hates himself for his offence,
She desperate with her nails her flesh doth tear.
He faintly flies sweating with guilty fear;
 She stays exclaiming on the direful night,
 He runs and chides his vanish'd loath'd delight.

He thence departs a heavy convertite,
She there remains a hopeless cast-away,
He in his speed looks for the morning light:
She prays she never may behold the day.
For day, quoth she, night's scapes doth open lay,
 And my true eyes have never practis'd how
 To cloak offences with a cunning brow.

They think not but that every eye can see,
The same disgrace which they themselves behold:
And therefore would they still in darkness be,
To have their unseen sin remain untold.
For they their guilt with weeping will unfold,
 And grave like water that doth eat in steel,
 Upon my cheeks, what helpless shame I feel.

Here she exclaims against repose and rest,
And bids her eyes hereafter still be blind,
She wakes her heart by beating on her breast,
And bids it leap from thence, where it may find
Some purer chest, to close so pure a mind.
　　Frantic with grief thus breathes she forth her spite,
　　Against the unseen secrecy of night.

O comfort-killing night, image of Hell,
Dim register, and notary of shame,
Black stage for tragedies, and murthers fell,
Vast sin-concealing Chaos, nurse of blame.
Blind muffled bawd, dark harbour for defame,
　　Grim cave of death, whispring conspirator,
　　With close-tongu'd treason and the ravisher.

O hateful, vaporous, and foggy night,
Since thou art guilty of my cureless crime:
Muster thy mists to meet the eastern light,
Make war against proportion'd course of time.
Or if thou wilt permit the Sun to climb
　　His wonted height, yet ere he go to bed,
　　Knit poisonous clouds about his golden head.

With rotten damps ravish the morning air,
Let their exhal'd unwholesome breaths make sick
The life of purity, the supreme fair,
Ere he arrive his weary noon-tide prick,
And let thy musty vapours march so thick,
　　That in their smoky ranks, his smother'd light
　　May set at noon, and make perpetual night.

Were Tarquin night, as he is but night's child,
The silver shining Queen he would disdain;
Her twinkling handmaids too (by him defil'd)
Through night's black bosom should not peep again.
So should I have co-partners in my pain,
   And fellowship in woe doth woe assuage,
   As Palmers' chat makes short their pilgrimage.

Where now I have no one to blush with me,
To cross their arms and hang their heads with mine,
To mask their brows and hide their infamy,
But I alone, alone must sit and pine,
Seasoning the earth with showers of silver brine;
   Mingling my talk with tears, my grief with groans,
   Poor wasting monuments of lasting moans.

O night thou furnace of foul reeking smoke!
Let not the jealous day behold that face,
Which underneath thy black all-hiding cloak
Immodestly lies martyr'd with disgrace.
Keep still possession of thy gloomy place,
   That all the faults which in thy reign are made,
   May likewise be sepulchred in thy shade.

Make me not object to the tell-tale day,
The light will show character'd in my brow,
The story of sweet chastity's decay,
The impious breach of holy wedlock vow.
Yea the illiterate that know not how
   To cipher what is writ in learned books,
   Will cote my loathsome trespass in my looks.

The nurse to still her child will tell my story,
And fright her crying babe with Tarquin's name.
The Orator to deck his oratory,
Will couple my reproach to Tarquin's shame.
Feast-finding minstrels tuning my defame,
    Will tie the hearers to attend each line,
    How Tarquin wronged me, I Colatine.

Let my good name, that senseless reputation,
For Colatine's dear love be kept unspotted:
If that be made a theme for disputation,
The branches of another root are rotted;
And undeserv'd reproach to him allotted,
    That is as clear from this attaint of mine,
    As I ere this was pure to Colatine.

O unseen shame, invisible disgrace,
O unfelt sore, crest-wounding private scar!
Reproach is stamp'd in Colatinus' face,
And Tarquin's eye may read the mot afar,
"How he in peace is wounded, not in war,
    Alas, how many bear such shameful blows,
    Which not themselves but he that gives them knows.

If Colatine, thine honour lay in me,
From me by strong assault it is bereft:
My honey lost, and I a drone-like bee,
Have no perfection of my summer left,
But robb'd and ransack'd by injurious theft.
    In thy weak hive a wandring wasp hath crept,
    And suck'd the honey which thy chaste bee kept.

Yet am I guilty of thy honour's wrack,
Yet for thy Honour did I entertain him,
Coming from thee I could not put him back:
For it had been dishonour to disdain him,
Besides of weariness he did complain him,
  And talk'd of Virtue (O unlook'd for evil),
  When Virtue is profan'd in such a Devil.

Why should the worm intrude the maiden bud?
Or hateful cuckoos hatch in sparrows' nests?
Or toads infect fair founts with venom mud?
Or tyrant folly lurk in gentle breasts?
Or Kings be breakers of their own behests?
  "But no perfection is so absolute,
  That some impurity doth not pollute.

The aged man that coffers up his gold,
Is plagu'd with cramps, and gouts, and painful fits,
And scarce hath eyes his treasure to behold,
But like still pining Tantalus he sits,
And useless barns the harvest of his wits:
  Having no other pleasure of his gain,
  But torment that it cannot cure his pain.

So then he hath it when he cannot use it,
And leaves it to be master'd by his young:
Who in their pride do presently abuse it,
Their father was too weak, and they too strong
To hold their cursed-blessed fortune long.
  "The sweets we wish for, turn to loathed sours,
  "Even in the moment that we call them ours.

Unruly blasts wait on the tender spring,
Unwholesome weeds take root with precious flowers,
The adder hisses where the sweet birds sing,
What Virtue breeds Iniquity devours:
We have no good that we can say is ours,
    But ill-annexed opportunity
    Or kills his life, or else his quality.

O opportunity thy guilt is great,
'Tis thou that execut'st the traitor's treason:
Thou sets the wolf where he the lamb may get,
Whoever plots the sin thou point'st the season.
'Tis thou that spurn'st at right, at law, at reason,
    And in thy shady cell where none may spy him,
    Sits sin to seize the souls that wander by him.

Thou makest the vestal violate her oath,
Thou blow'st the fire when temperance is thaw'd,
Thou smother'st honesty, thou murth'rest troth,
Thou foul abettor, thou notorious bawd,
Thou plantest scandal, and displacest laud.
    Thou ravisher, thou traitor, thou false thief,
    Thy honey turns to gall, thy joy to grief.

Thy secret pleasure turns to open shame,
Thy private feasting to a public fast,
Thy smoothing titles to a ragged name,
Thy sugred tongue to bitter wormwood taste,
Thy violent vanities can never last.
    How comes it then, vile opportunity
    Being so bad, such numbers seek for thee?

When wilt thou be the humble suppliant's friend
And bring him where his suit may be obtained?
When wilt thou sort an hour great strifes to end?
Or free that soul which wretchedness hath chained?
Give physic to the sick, ease to the pained?
   The poor, lame, blind, halt, creep, cry out for thee,
   But they ne'er meet with opportunity.

The patient dies while the physician sleeps,
The orphan pines while the oppressor feeds.
Justice is feasting while the widow weeps.
Advice is sporting while infection breeds.
Thou grant'st no time for charitable deeds.
   Wrath, envy, treason, rape, and murther's rages,
   Thy heinous hours wait on them as their pages.

When Truth and Virtue have to do with thee,
A thousand crosses keep them from thy aid:
They buy thy help, but sin ne'er gives a fee,
He gratis comes, and thou art well appaid,
As well to hear, as grant what he hath said.
   My Colatine would else have come to me,
   When Tarquin did, but he was stay'd by thee.

Guilty thou art of murther, and of theft,
Guilty of perjury, and subornation,
Guilty of treason, forgery, and shift,
Guilty of incest that abomination,
An accessary by thine inclination,
   To all sins past and all that are to come,
   From the creation to the general doom.

D

Mis-shapen time, copesmate of ugly night,
Swift subtle post, carrier of grisly care,
Eater of youth, false slave to false delight:
Base watch of woes, sin's packhorse, virtue's snare.
Thou nursest all, and murthrest all that are.
   O hear me then, injurious shifting time,
   Be guilty of my death since of my crime.

Why hath thy servant opportunity
Betray'd the hours thou gav'st me to repose?
Cancell'd my fortunes, and enchained me
To endless date of never-ending woes?
Time's office is to fine the hate of foes,
   To eat up errors by opinion bred,
   Not spend the dowry of a lawful bed.

Time's glory is to calm contending Kings,
To unmask falsehood, and bring truth to light,
To stamp the seal of time in aged things,
To wake the morn, and sentinel the night,
To wrong the wronger till he render right,
   To ruinate proud buildings with thy hours,
   And smear with dust their glitt'ring golden towers.

To fill with worm-holes stately monuments,
To feed oblivion with decay of things,
To blot old books, and alter their contents,
To pluck the quills from ancient ravens' wings,
To dry the old oak's sap, and cherish springs:
   To spoil antiquities of hammer'd steel,
   And turn the giddy round of Fortune's wheel.

To show the beldame daughters of her daughter,
To make the child a man, the man a child,
To slay the tiger that doth live by slaughter,
To tame the unicorn, and lion wild,
To mock the subtle in themselves beguil'd,
   To cheer the ploughman with increaseful crops,
   And waste huge stones with little water drops.

Why work'st thou mischief in thy pilgrimage,
Unless thou couldst return to make amends?
One poor retiring minute in an age
Would purchase thee a thousand thousand friends,
Lending him wit that to bad debtors lends,
   O this dread night, wouldst thou one hour come back,
   I could prevent this storm, and shun thy wrack.

Thou ceaseless lackey to Eternity,
With some mischance cross Tarquin in his flight.
Devise extremes beyond extremity,
To make him curse this cursed crimeful night:
Let ghastly shadows his lewd eyes affright,
   And the dire thought of his committed evil,
   Shape every bush a hideous shapeless devil.

Disturb his hours of rest with restless trances,
Afflict him in his bed with bedrid groans,
Let there bechance him pitiful mischances,
To make him moan, but pity not his moans:
Stone him with harden'd hearts harder than stones,
   And let mild women to him lose their mildness,
   Wilder to him than tigers in their wildness.

Let him have time to tear his curled hair,
Let him have time against himself to rave,
Let him have time of time's help to despair,
Let him have time to live a loathed slave,
Let him have time a beggar's orts to crave,
    And time to see one that by alms doth live,
    Disdain to him disdained scraps to give.

Let him have time to see his friends his foes,
And merry fools to mock at him resort:
Let him have time to mark how slow time goes
In time of sorrow, and how swift and short
His time of folly, and his time of sport.
    And ever let his unrecalling crime
    Have time to wail th' abusing of his time.

O time thou tutor both to good and bad,
Teach me to curse him that thou taught'st this ill:
At his own shadow let the thief run mad,
Himself, himself seek every hour to kill,
Such wretched hands such wretched blood should spill.
    For who so base would such an office have,
    As slanderous deaths-man to so base a slave.

The baser is he coming from a King,
To shame his hope with deeds degenerate,
The mightier man the mightier is the thing
That makes him honour'd, or begets him hate:
For greatest scandal waits on greatest state.
    The Moon being clouded, presently is miss'd,
    But little stars may hide them when they list.

The crow may bathe his coal-black wings in mire,
And unperceiv'd fly with the filth away,
But if the like the snow-white swan desire,
The stain upon his silver down will stay.
Poor grooms are sightless night, kings glorious day,
  Gnats are unnoted wheresoe'er they fly,
  But eagles gaz'd upon with every eye.

Out idle words, servants to shallow fools,
Unprofitable sounds, weak arbitrators,
Busy yourselves in skill-contending schools,
Debate where leisure serves with dull debaters:
To trembling clients be you mediators,
  For me, I force not argument a straw,
  Since that my case is past the help of law.

In vain I rail at opportunity,
At time, at Tarquin, and uncheerful night,
In vain I cavil with mine infamy,
In vain I spurn at my confirm'd despite,
This helpless smoke of words doth me no right:
  The remedy indeed to do me good,
  Is to let forth my foul defiled blood.

Poor hand why quiver'st thou at this decree?
Honour thyself to rid me of this shame,
For if I die, my Honour lives in thee,
But if I live thou liv'st in my defame;
Since thou couldst not defend thy loyal Dame,
  And wast afeard to scratch her wicked foe,
  Kill both thyself, and her for yielding so.

This said, from her betumbled couch she starteth,
To find some desprat instrument of death,
But this no slaughterhouse no tool imparteth,
To make more vent for passage of her breath,
Which thronging through her lips so vanisheth,
   As smoke from Etna, that in air consumes,
   Or that which from discharged cannon fumes.

In vain (quoth she) I live, and seek in vain
Some happy mean to end a hapless life.
I feared by Tarquin's falchion to be slain,
Yet for the self same purpose seek a knife;
But when I fear'd I was a loyal wife,
   So am I now, o no that cannot be,
   Of that true type hath Tarquin rifled me.

O that is gone for which I sought to live,
And therefore now I need not fear to die,
To clear this spot by death (at least) I give
A badge of Fame to slander's livery,
A dying life, to living infamy:
   Poor helpless help, the treasure stol'n away,
   To burn the guiltless casket where it lay.

Well well dear Colatine, thou shalt not know
The stained taste of violated troth:
I will not wrong thy true affection so,
To flatter thee with an infringed oath:
This bastard graff shall never come to growth,
   He shall not boast who did thy stock pollute,
   That thou art doting father of his fruit.

Nor shall he smile at thee in secret thought,
Nor laugh with his companions at thy state,
But thou shalt know thy int'rest was not bought
Basely with gold, but stol'n from forth thy gate.
For me I am the mistress of my fate,
   And with my trespass never will dispense,
   Till life to death acquit my forc'd offence.

I will not poison thee with my attaint,
Nor fold my fault in cleanly-coin'd excuses,
My sable ground of sin I will not paint,
To hide the truth of this false night's abuses.
My tongue shall utter all, mine eyes like sluices,
   As from a mountain spring that feeds a dale,
   Shall gush pure streams to purge my impure tale.

By this lamenting Philomele had ended
The well-tun'd warble of her nightly sorrow,
And solemn night with slow sad gait descended
To ugly Hell, when lo the blushing morrow
Lends light to all fair eyes that light will borrow.
   But cloudy Lucrece shames herself to see,
   And therefore still in night would cloister'd be.

Revealing day through every cranny spies,
And seems to point her out where she sits weeping,
To whom she sobbing speaks, o eye of eyes,
Why pry'st thou through my window? leave thy peeping,
Mock with thy tickling beams, eyes that are sleeping;
   Brand not my forehead with thy piercing light,
   For day hath nought to do what's done by night.

Thus cavils she with every thing she sees,
True grief is fond and testy as a child,
Who wayward once, his mood with nought agrees,
Old woes, not infant sorrows bear them mild,
Continuance tames the one, the other wild,
    Like an unpractis'd swimmer plunging still,
    With too much labour drowns for want of skill.

So she deep drenched in a sea of care,
Holds disputation with each thing she views,
And to herself all sorrow doth compare,
No object but her passion's strength renews:
And as one shifts another straight ensues,
    Sometime her grief is dumb and hath no words,
    Sometime 'tis mad and too much talk affords.

The little birds that tune their morning's joy,
Make her moans mad, with their sweet melody,
"For mirth doth search the bottom of annoy,
"Sad souls are slain in merry company,
"Grief best is pleas'd with grief's society;
    "True sorrow then is feelingly suffic'd,
    "When with like semblance it is sympathiz'd.

"'Tis double death to drown in ken of shore,
"He ten times pines, that pines beholding food,
"To see the salve doth make the wound ache more:
"Great grief grieves most at that would do it good;
"Deep woes roll forward like a gentle flood,
    Who being stopp'd, the bounding banks o'erflows,
    Grief dallied with, nor law, nor limit knows.

You mocking birds (quoth she) your tunes entomb
Within your hollow swelling feather'd breasts,
And in my hearing be you mute and dumb,
My restless discord loves no stops nor rests:
"A woeful Hostess brooks not merry guests.
    Relish your nimble notes to pleasing ears,
    "Distress likes dumps when time is kept with tears.

Come Philomele that sing'st of ravishment,
Make thy sad grove in my dishevell'd hair,
As the dank earth weeps at thy languishment:
So I at each sad strain, will strain a tear,
And with deep groans the diapason bear:
    For burthen-wise I'll hum on Tarquin still,
    While thou on Tereus descants better skill.

And whiles against a thorn thou bear'st thy part,
To keep thy sharp woes waking, wretched I
To imitate thee well, against my heart
Will fix a sharp knife to affright mine eye,
Who if it wink shall thereon fall and die.
    These means as frets upon an instrument,
    Shall tune our heart-strings to true languishment.

And for poor bird thou sing'st not in the day,
As shaming any eye should thee behold:
Some dark deep desert seated from the way,
That knows not parching heat, nor freezing cold
Will we find out: and there we will unfold
    To creatures stern, sad tunes to change their kinds,
    Since men prove beasts, let beasts bear gentle minds.

As the poor frighted deer that stands at gaze,
Wildly determining which way to fly,
Or one encompass'd with a winding maze,
That cannot tread the way out readily:
So with herself is she in mutiny,
  To live or die which of the twin were better,
  When life is sham'd and death reproach's debtor.

To kill myself, quoth she, alack what were it,
But with my body my poor soul's pollution?
They that lose half with greater patience bear it,
Than they whose whole is swallow'd in confusion.
That mother tries a merciless conclusion,
  Who having two sweet babes, when death takes one,
  Will slay the other, and be nurse to none.

My body or my soul which was the dearer?
When the one pure, the other made divine,
Whose love of either to myself was nearer?
When both were kept for Heaven and Colatine:
Ay me, the bark pill'd from the lofty pine,
  His leaves will wither, and his sap decay,
  So must my soul her bark being pill'd away.

Her house is sack'd, her quiet interrupted,
Her mansion batter'd by the enemy,
Her sacred temple spotted, spoil'd, corrupted,
Grossly engirt with daring infamy.
Then let it not be call'd impiety,
  If in this blemish'd fort I make some hole,
  Through which I may convey this troubled soul.

Yet die I will not, till my Colatine
Have heard the cause of my untimely death,
That he may vow in that sad hour of mine,
Revenge on him that made me stop my breath,
My stained blood to Tarquin I'll bequeath,
    Which by him tainted, shall for him be spent,
    And as his due writ in my testament.

My Honour I'll bequeath unto the knife
That wounds my body so dishonoured,
'Tis Honour to deprive dishonour'd life,
The one will live, the other being dead.
So of shame's ashes shall my Fame be bred,
    For in my death I murther shameful scorn,
    My shame so dead, mine honour is new born.

Dear Lord of that dear jewel I have lost,
What legacy shall I bequeath to thee?
My resolution love shall be thy boast,
By whose example thou reveng'd mayst be.
How Tarquin must be us'd, read it in me,
    Myself thy friend will kill myself thy foe,
    And for my sake serve thou false Tarquin so.

This brief abridgement of my will I make,
My soul and body to the skies and ground:
My resolution Husband do thou take,
Mine Honour be the knife's that makes my wound,
My shame be his that did my Fame confound;
    And all my Fame that lives disbursed be,
    To those that live and think no shame of me.

Thou Colatine shalt oversee this will,
How was I over seen that thou shalt see it?
My blood shall wash the slander of mine ill,
My life's foul deed my life's fair end shall free it.
Faint not faint heart, but stoutly say so be it,
    Yield to my hand, my hand shall conquer thee,
    Thou dead, both die, and both shall victors be.

This plot of death when sadly she had laid,
And wip'd the brinish pearl from her bright eyes,
With untun'd tongue she hoarsely calls her maid,
Whose swift obedience to her mistress hies.
"For fleet-wing'd duty with thought's feathers flies,
    Poor Lucrece' cheeks unto her maid seem so,
    As winter meads when sun doth melt their snow.

Her mistress she doth give demure good morrow,
With soft slow tongue, true mark of modesty,
And sorts a sad look to her Lady's sorrow,
(For why her face wore sorrow's livery).
But durst not ask of her audaciously,
    Why her two suns were cloud eclipsed so,
    Nor why her fair cheeks over-wash'd with woe.

But as the earth doth weep the Sun being set,
Each flower moisten'd like a melting eye:
Even so the maid with swelling drops 'gan wet
Her circled eyne enforc'd, by sympathy
Of those fair suns set in her mistress' sky,
    Who in a salt-wav'd Ocean quench their light,
    Which makes the maid weep like the dewy night.

A pretty while these pretty creatures stand,
Like ivory conduits coral cisterns filling:
One justly weeps, the other takes in hand
No cause, but company of her drops spilling.
Their gentle sex to weep are often willing,
  Grieving themselves to guess at others' smarts,
  And then they drown their eyes, or break their hearts.

For men have marble, women waxen minds,
And therefore are they form'd as marble will,
The weak oppress'd, the impression of strange kinds
Is form'd in them by force, by fraud, or skill.
Then call them not the authors of their ill,
  No more than wax shall be accounted evil,
  Wherein is stamp'd the semblance of a Devil.

Their smoothness, like a goodly champaign plain,
Lays open all the little worms that creep,
In men as in a rough grown grove remain,
Cave-keeping evils that obscurely sleep.
Through crystal walls each little mote will peep,
  Though men can cover crimes with bold stern looks,
  Poor women's faces are their own faults' books.

No man inveigh against the withered flower,
But chide rough winter that the flower hath kill'd,
Not that devour'd, but that which doth devour
Is worthy blame, o let it not be hild
Poor women's faults, that they are so fulfill'd
  With men's abuses, those proud Lords to blame,
  Make weak-made women tenants to their shame.

The precedent whereof in Lucrece' view,
Assail'd by night with circumstances strong
Of present death, and shame that might ensue,
By that her death to do her husband wrong.
Such danger to resistance did belong:
   That dying fear through all her body spread,
   And who cannot abuse a body dead?

By this mild patience bid fair Lucrece speak,
To the poor counterfeit of her complaining,
My girl, quoth she, on what occasion break
Those tears from thee, that down thy cheeks are raining?
If thou dost weep for grief of my sustaining:
   Know gentle wench it small avails my mood,
   If tears could help, mine own would do me good.

But tell me girl, when went (and there she stay'd,
Till after a deep groan) Tarquin from hence.
Madam ere I was up (replied the maid),
The more to blame my sluggard negligence.
Yet with the fault I thus far can dispense:
   Myself was stirring ere the break of day,
   And ere I rose was Tarquin gone away.

But Lady, if your maid may be so bold,
She would request to know your heaviness:
(O peace quoth Lucrece) if it should be told,
The repetition cannot make it less:
For more it is, than I can well express,
   And that deep torture may be call'd a Hell,
   When more is felt than one hath power to tell.

Go get me hither paper, ink, and pen,
Yet save that labour, for I have them here.
(What should I say) one of my husband's men
Bid thou be ready, by and by, to bear
A letter to my Lord, my Love, my Dear,
    Bid him with speed prepare to carry it,
    The cause craves haste, and it will soon be writ.

Her maid is gone, and she prepares to write,
First hovering o'er the paper with her quill:
Conceit and grief an eager combat fight,
What wit sets down is blotted straight with will.
This is too curious good, this blunt and ill,
    Much like a press of people at the door,
    Throng her inventions which shall go before.

At last she thus begins: Thou worthy Lord,
Of that unworthy wife that greeteth thee,
Health to thy person, next, vouchsafe t' afford
(If ever love, thy Lucrece thou wilt see),
Some present speed, to come and visit me:
    So I commend me, from our house in grief,
    My woes are tedious, though my words are brief.

Here folds she up the tenor of her woe,
Her certain sorrow writ uncertainly,
By this short schedule Colatine may know
Her grief, but not her grief's true quality,
She dares not thereof make discovery,
    Lest he should hold it her own gross abuse,
    Ere she with blood had stain'd her stain'd excuse.

Besides the life and feeling of her passion,
She hoards to spend, when he is by to hear her,
When sighs, and groans, and tears may grace the fashion
Of her disgrace, the better so to clear her
From that suspicion which the world might bear her.
 To shun this blot, she would not blot the letter
 With words, till action might become them better.

To see sad sights, moves more than hear them told,
For then the eye interprets to the ear
The heavy motion that it doth behold,
When every part, a part of woe doth bear.
'Tis but a part of sorrow that we hear,
 Deep sounds make lesser noise than shallow fords,
 And sorrow ebbs, being blown with wind of words.

Her letter now is seal'd, and on it writ
At Ardea to my Lord with more than haste.
The Post attends, and she delivers it,
Charging the sour-fac'd groom, to hie as fast
As lagging fowls before the northern blasts,
 Speed more than speed, but dull and slow she deems,
 Extremity still urgeth such extremes.

The homely villain cursies to her low,
And blushing on her with a steadfast eye,
Receives the scroll without or yea or no,
And forth with bashful innocence doth hie.
But they whose guilt within their bosoms lie,
 Imagine every eye beholds their blame,
 For Lucrece thought, he blush'd to see her shame.

When silly groom (God wot) it was defect
Of spirit, life, and bold audacity,
Such harmless creatures have a true respect
To talk in deeds, while others saucily
Promise more speed, but do it leisurely.
    Even so this pattern of the worn-out age,
    Pawn'd honest looks, but laid no words to gage.

His kindled duty kindled her mistrust,
That two red fires in both their faces blazed,
She thought he blush'd, as knowing Tarquin's lust,
And blushing with him, wistly on him gazed,
Her earnest eye did make him more amazed.
    The more she saw the blood his cheeks replenish,
    The more she thought he spied in her some blemish.

But long she thinks till he return again,
And yet the duteous vassal scarce is gone,
The weary time she cannot entertain,
For now 'tis stale to sigh, to weep, and groan,
So woe hath wearied woe, moan tired moan,
    That she her plaints a little while doth stay,
    Pausing for means to mourn some newer way.

At last she calls to mind where hangs a piece
Of skilful painting, made for Priam's Troy,
Before the which is drawn the power of Greece,
For Helen's rape, the City to destroy,
Threatning cloud-kissing Ilion with annoy,
    Which the conceited Painter drew so proud,
    As Heaven (it seem'd) to kiss the turrets bow'd.

A thousand lamentable objects there,
In scorn of Nature, Art gave lifeless life,
Many a dry drop seem'd a weeping tear,
Shed for the slaughter'd husband by the wife.
The red blood reek'd to show the Painter's strife,
    And dying eyes gleam'd forth their ashy lights,
    Like dying coals burnt out in tedious nights.

There might you see the labouring pioner
Begrim'd with sweat, and smeared all with dust,
And from the towers of Troy, there would appear
The very eyes of men through loop-holes thrust,
Gazing upon the Greeks with little lust,
    Such sweet observance in this work was had,
    That one might see those far off eyes look sad.

In great commanders, Grace, and Majesty,
You might behold triumphing in their faces,
In youth quick-bearing and dexterity,
And here and there the Painter interlaces
Pale cowards marching on with trembling paces.
    Which heartless peasants did so well resemble,
    That one would swear he saw them quake and tremble.

In Ajax and Ulysses, o what Art
Of physiognomy might one behold!
The face of either cipher'd either's heart,
Their face, their manners most expressly told,
In Ajax's eyes blunt rage and rigour roll'd,
    But the mild glance that sly Ulysses lent,
    Show'd deep regard and smiling government.

There pleading might you see grave Nestor stand,
As 'twere encouraging the Greeks to fight,
Making such sober action with his hand,
That it beguil'd attention, charm'd the sight,
In speech it seem'd his beard, all silver white,
   Wagg'd up and down, and from his lips did fly,
   Thin winding breath which purl'd up to the sky.

About him were a press of gaping faces,
Which seem'd to swallow up his sound advice,
All jointly listning, but with several graces,
As if some Marmaid did their ears entice,
Some high, some low, the Painter was so nice.
   The scalps of many, almost hid behind,
   To jump up higher seem'd to mock the mind.

Here one man's hand lean'd on another's head,
His nose being shadow'd by his neighbour's ear,
Here one being throng'd, bears back all boll'n, and red,
Another smother'd, seems to pelt and swear,
And in their rage such signs of rage they bear,
   As but for loss of Nestor's golden words,
   It seem'd they would debate with angry swords.

For much imaginary work was there,
Conceit deceitful, so compact so kind,
That for Achilles' image stood his spear
Grip'd in an armed hand, himself behind
Was left unseen, save to the eye of mind,
   A hand, a foot, a face, a leg, a head,
   Stood for the whole to be imagined.

And from the walls of strong besieged Troy,
When their brave hope, bold Hector march'd to field,
Stood many Trojan mothers sharing joy,
To see their youthful sons bright weapons wield,
And to their hope they such odd action yield,
    That through their light joy seemed to appear,
    (Like bright things stain'd) a kind of heavy fear.

And from the strand of Dardan where they fought,
To Simois' reddy banks the red blood ran,
Whose waves to imitate the battle sought
With swelling ridges, and their ranks began
To break upon the galled shore, and than
    Retire again, till meeting greater ranks
    They join, and shoot their foam at Simois' banks.

To this well painted piece is Lucrece come,
To find a face where all distress is stell'd,
Many she sees, where cares have carved some,
But none where all distress and dolour dwell'd,
Till she despairing Hecuba beheld,
    Staring on Priam's wounds with her old eyes,
    Which bleeding under Pyrrhus' proud foot lies.

In her the Painter had anathomiz'd
Time's ruin, beauty's wrack, and grim care's reign,
Her cheeks with chops and wrinkles were disguis'd,
Of what she was, no semblance did remain:
Her blue blood chang'd to black in every vein,
    Wanting the spring, that those shrunk pipes had fed,
    Show'd life imprison'd in a body dead.

On this sad shadow Lucrece spends her eyes,
And shapes her sorrow to the Beldame's woes,
Who nothing wants to answer her but cries,
And bitter words to ban her cruel foes.
The Painter was no God to lend her those,
    And therefore Lucrece swears he did her wrong,
    To give her so much grief, and not a tongue.

Poor instrument (quoth she) without a sound,
I'll tune thy woes with my lamenting tongue,
And drop sweet balm in Priam's painted wound,
And rail on Pyrrhus that hath done him wrong;
And with my tears quench Troy that burns so long;
    And with my knife scratch out the angry eyes,
    Of all the Greeks that are thine enemies.

Show me the strumpet that began this stir,
That with my nails her beauty I may tear:
Thy heat of lust fond Paris did incur
This load of wrath, that burning Troy doth bear;
Thy eye kindled the fire that burneth here,
    And here in Troy for trespass of thine eye,
    The Sire, the son, the Dame and daughter die.

Why should the private pleasure of some one
Become the public plague of many moe?
Let sin alone committed, light alone
Upon his head that hath transgressed so.
Let guiltless souls be freed from guilty woe,
    For one's offence why should so many fall?
    To plague a private sin in general.

Lo here weeps Hecuba, here Priam dies,
Here manly Hector faints, here Troylus sounds;
Here friend by friend in bloody channel lies:
And friend to friend gives unadvised wounds,
And one man's lust these many lives confounds.
     Had doting Priam check'd his son's desire,
       Troy had been bright with fame, and not with fire.

Here feelingly she weeps Troy's painted woes,
For sorrow, like a heavy hanging bell,
Once set on ringing, with his own weight goes,
Then little strength rings out the doleful knell,
So Lucrece set a-work, sad tales doth tell
     To pencill'd pensiveness, and colour'd sorrow,
       She lends them words, and she their looks doth borrow.

She throws her eyes about the painting round,
And who she finds forlorn, she doth lament:
At last she sees a wretched image bound,
That piteous looks, to Phrygian shepherds lent,
His face though full of cares, yet show'd content,
     Onward to Troy with the blunt swains he goes,
       So mild that patience seem'd to scorn his woes.

In him the Painter labour'd with his skill
To hide deceit, and give the harmless show
An humble gait, calm looks, eyes wailing still,
A brow unbent that seem'd to welcome woe,
Cheeks neither red, nor pale, but mingled so,
     That blushing red, no guilty instance gave,
       Nor ashy pale, the fear that false hearts have.

But like a constant and confirmed Devil,
He entertain'd a show, so seeming just,
And therein so ensconc'd his secret evil,
That Jealousy itself could not mistrust,
False creeping Craft and Perjury should thrust
  Into so bright a day, such blackfac'd storms,
  Or blot with Hell-born sin such saint-like forms.

The well-skill'd workman this mild image drew
For perjur'd Sinon, whose enchanting story
The credulous old Priam after slew.
Whose words like wildfire burnt the shining glory
Of rich-built Ilion, that the skies were sorry,
  And little stars shot from their fixed places,
  When their glass fell, wherein they view'd their faces.

This picture she advisedly perus'd,
And chid the Painter for his wondrous skill:
Saying, some shape in Sinon's was abus'd,
So fair a form lodg'd not a mind so ill,
And still on him she gaz'd, and gazing still,
  Such signs of truth in his plain face she spied,
  That she concludes, the picture was belied.

It cannot be (quoth she) that so much guile
(She would have said) can lurk in such a look:
But Tarquin's shape, came in her mind the while,
And from her tongue, can lurk, from cannot, took
It cannot be, she in that sense forsook,
  And turn'd it thus, it cannot be I find,
  But such a face should bear a wicked mind.

For even as subtle Sinon here is painted,
So sober sad, so weary, and so mild,
(As if with grief or travail he had fainted)
To me came Tarquin armed to beguild
With outward honesty, but yet defil'd
    With inward vice, as Priam him did cherish:
    So did I Tarquin, so my Troy did perish.

Look look how listning Priam wets his eyes,
To see those borrow'd tears that Sinon sheds,
Priam why art thou old, and yet not wise?
For every tear he falls a Trojan bleeds:
His eye drops fire, no water thence proceeds,
    Those round clear pearls of his that move thy pity,
    Are balls of quenchless fire to burn thy City.

Such Devils steal effects from lightless Hell,
For Sinon in his fire doth quake with cold,
And in that cold hot burning fire doth dwell,
These contraries such unity do hold,
Only to flatter fools, and make them bold,
    So Priam's trust false Sinon's tears doth flatter,
    That he finds means to burn his Troy with water.

Here all enrag'd such passion her assails,
That patience is quite beaten from her breast,
She tears the senseless Sinon with her nails,
Comparing him to that unhappy guest,
Whose deed hath made herself, herself detest,
    At last she smilingly with this gives o'er,
    Fool fool, quoth she, his wounds will not be sore.

Thus ebbs and flows the current of her sorrow,
And time doth weary time with her complaining,
She looks for night, and then she longs for morrow,
And both she thinks too long with her remaining.
Short time seems long, in sorrow's sharp sustaining,
    Though woe be heavy, yet it seldom sleeps,
    And they that watch, see time, how slow it creeps.

Which all this time hath overslipp'd her thought,
That she with painted images hath spent,
Being from the feeling of her own grief brought,
By deep surmise of others' detriment,
Losing her woes in shows of discontent:
    It easeth some, though none it ever cured,
    To think their dolour others have endured.

But now the mindful messenger come back,
Brings home his Lord and other company,
Who finds his Lucrece clad in mourning black,
And round about her tear-distained eye
Blue circles stream'd, like rainbows in the sky.
    These watergalls in her dim element,
    Foretell new storms to those already spent.

Which when her sad beholding husband saw,
Amazedly in her sad face he stares:
Her eyes though sod in tears look'd red and raw,
Her lively colour kill'd with deadly cares,
He hath no power to ask her how she fares,
    Both stood like old acquaintance in a trance,
    Met far from home, wondring each other's chance.

At last he takes her by the bloodless hand,
And thus begins: what uncouth ill event
Hath thee befall'n, that thou dost trembling stand?
Sweet love what spite hath thy fair colour spent?
Why art thou thus attir'd in discontent?
    Unmask dear dear, this moody heaviness,
    And tell thy grief, that we may give redress.

Three times with sighs she gives her sorrow fire,
Ere once she can discharge one word of woe:
At length address'd to answer his desire,
She modestly prepares, to let them know
Her Honour is ta'en prisoner by the Foe,
    While Colatine and his consorted Lords,
    With sad attention long to hear her words.

And now this pale Swan in her watery nest,
Begins the sad dirge of her certain ending,
Few words (quoth she) shall fit the trespass best,
Where no excuse can give the fault amending.
In me moe woes than words are now depending,
    And my laments would be drawn out too long,
    To tell them all with one poor tired tongue.

Then be this all the task it hath to say,
Dear husband in the interest of thy bed
A stranger came, and on that pillow lay,
Where thou wast wont to rest thy weary head,
And what wrong else may be imagined,
    By foul enforcement might be done to me,
    From that (alas) thy Lucrece is not free.

For in the dreadful dead of dark midnight,
With shining falchion in my chamber came
A creeping creature with a flaming light,
And softly cried, awake thou Roman Dame,
And entertain my love, else lasting shame
  On thee and thine this night I will inflict,
  If thou my love's desire do contradict.

For some hard favour'd groom of thine, quoth he,
Unless thou yoke thy liking to my will
I'll murther straight, and then I'll slaughter thee,
And swear I found you where you did fulfil
The loathsome act of lust, and so did kill
  The lechers in their deed, this act will be
  My fame, and thy perpetual infamy.

With this, I did begin to start and cry,
And then against my heart he set his sword,
Swearing, unless I took all patiently,
I should not live to speak another word.
So should my shame still rest upon record,
  And never be forgot in mighty Rome
  Th' adulterate death of Lucrece, and her groom.

Mine enemy was strong, my poor self weak,
(And far the weaker with so strong a fear)
My bloody Judge forbod my tongue to speak,
No rightful plea might plead for Justice there.
His scarlet Lust came evidence to swear
  That my poor beauty had purloin'd his eyes,
  And when the Judge is robb'd, the prisoner dies.

O teach me how to make mine own excuse,
Or (at the least) this refuge let me find,
Though my gross blood be stain'd with this abuse,
Immaculate, and spotless is my mind,
That was not forc'd, that never was inclin'd
  To accessary yieldings, but still pure
  Doth in her poison'd closet yet endure.

Lo here the hopeless Merchant of this loss,
With head declin'd, and voice damm'd up with woe,
With sad set eyes and wretched arms across,
From lips new waxen pale, begins to blow
The grief away, that stops his answer so.
  But wretched as he is he strives in vain,
  What he breathes out, his breath drinks up again.

As through an arch, the violent roaring tide,
Outruns the eye that doth behold his haste:
Yet in the eddy boundeth in his pride,
Back to the strait that forc'd him on so fast:
In rage sent out, recall'd in rage being past,
  Even so his sighs, his sorrows make a saw,
  To push grief on, and back the same grief draw.

Which speechless woe of his poor she attendeth,
And his untimely frenzy thus awaketh,
Dear Lord, thy sorrow to my sorrow lendeth
Another power, no flood by raining slaketh,
My woe too sensible thy passion maketh
  More feeling painful, let it then suffice
  To drown one woe, one pair of weeping eyes.

And for my sake when I might charm thee so,
For she that was thy Lucrece, now attend me,
Be suddenly revenged on my Foe.
Thine, mine, his own, suppose thou dost defend me
From what is past, the help that thou shalt lend me
  Comes all too late, yet let the Traitor die,
  "For sparing Justice feeds iniquity.

But ere I name him, you fair Lords, quoth she,
(Speaking to those that came with Colatine)
Shall plight your honourable faiths to me,
With swift pursuit to venge this wrong of mine,
For 'tis a meritorious fair design,
  To chase injustice with revengeful arms,
  Knights by their oaths should right poor Ladies' harms.

At this request, with noble disposition,
Each present Lord began to promise aid,
As bound in Knighthood to her imposition,
Longing to hear the hateful Foe bewray'd.
But she that yet her sad task hath not said,
  The protestation stops, o speak quoth she,
  How may this forced stain be wip'd from me?

What is the quality of my offence
Being constrain'd with dreadful circumstance?
May my pure mind with the foul act dispense
My low declined Honour to advance?
May any terms acquit me from this chance?
  The poison'd fountain clears itself again,
  And why not I from this compelled stain?

With this they all at once began to say,
Her body's stain, her mind untainted clears,
While with a joyless smile, she turns away
The face, that map which deep impression bears
Of hard misfortune, carv'd in it with tears.
    No no, quoth she, no Dame hereafter living,
    By my excuse shall claim excuse's giving.

Here with a sigh as if her heart would break,
She throws forth Tarquin's name: he he, she says.
But more than he, her poor tongue could not speak,
Till after many accents and delays,
Untimely breathings, sick and short assays,
    She utters this, he he fair Lords, 'tis he
    That guides this hand to give this wound to me.

Even here she sheathed in her harmless breast
A harmful knife, that thence her soul unsheathed,
That blow did bail it from the deep unrest
Of that polluted prison, where it breathed:
Her contrite sighs unto the clouds bequeathed
    Her winged sprite, and through her wounds doth fly
    Life's lasting date, from cancell'd destiny.

Stone still, astonish'd with this deadly deed,
Stood Colatine, and all his lordly crew,
Till Lucrece' Father that beholds her bleed,
Himself, on her self-slaughter'd body threw,
And from the purple fountain Brutus drew
    The murdrous knife, and as it left the place,
    Her blood in poor revenge, held it in chase.

And bubbling from her breast, it doth divide
In two slow rivers, that the crimson blood
Circles her body in on every side,
Who like a late sack'd Island vastly stood
Bare and unpeopled, in this fearful flood.
    Some of her blood still pure and red remain'd,
    And some look'd black, and that false Tarquin stain'd.

About the mourning and congealed face
Of that black blood, a watery rigol goes,
Which seems to weep upon the tainted place,
And ever since as pitying Lucrece' woes,
Corrupted blood, some watery token shows,
    And blood untainted, still doth red abide,
    Blushing at that which is so putrified.

Daughter, dear daughter, old Lucretius cries,
That life was mine which thou hast here deprived,
If in the child the father's image lies,
Where shall I live now Lucrece is unlived?
Thou wast not to this end from me derived.
    If children predecease progenitors,
    We are their offspring and they none of ours.

Poor broken glass, I often did behold
In thy sweet semblance, my old age new born,
But now that fair fresh mirror dim and old
Shows me a bare-bon'd death by time out-worn,
O from thy cheeks my image thou hast torn,
    And shiver'd all the beauty of my glass,
    That I no more can see what once I was.

O time cease thou thy course and last no longer,
If they surcease to be that should survive:
Shall rotten death make conquest of the stronger,
And leave the faltering feeble souls alive?
The old bees dies, the young possess their hive,
    Then live sweet Lucrece, live again and see
    Thy father die, and not thy father thee.

By this starts Colatine as from a dream,
And bids Lucretius give his sorrow place,
And then in key-cold Lucrece' bleeding stream
He falls, and bathes the pale fear in his face,
And counterfeits to die with her a space.
    Till manly shame bids him possess his breath,
    And live to be revenged on her death.

The deep vexation of his inward soul,
Hath serv'd a dumb arrest upon his tongue,
Who mad that sorrow should his use control,
Or keep him from heart-easing words so long,
Begins to talk, but through his lips do throng
    Weak words, so thick come in his poor heart's aid,
    That no man could distinguish what he said.

Yet sometime Tarquin was pronounced plain,
But through his teeth, as if the name he tore,
This windy tempest, till it blow up rain,
Held back his sorrow's tide, to make it more.
At last it rains, and busy winds give o'er,
    Then son and father weep with equal strife,
    Who should weep most for daughter or for wife.

The one doth call her his, the other his,
Yet neither may possess the claim they lay.
The father says, she's mine, o mine she is
Replies her husband, do not take away
My sorrow's interest, let no mourner say
    He weeps for her, for she was only mine,
    And only must be wail'd by Colatine.

O, quoth Lucretius, I did give that life
Which she too early and too late hath spill'd.
Woe woe, quoth Colatine, she was my wife,
I ow'd her, and 'tis mine that she hath kill'd.
My daughter and my wife with clamours fill'd
    The dispers'd air, who holding Lucrece' life,
    Answer'd their cries, my daughter and my wife.

Brutus who pluck'd the knife from Lucrece' side,
Seeing such emulation in their woe,
Began to clothe his wit in state and pride,
Burying in Lucrece' wound his folly's show,
He with the Romans was esteemed so
    As silly jeering idiots are with Kings,
    For sportive words, and uttring foolish things.

But now he throws that shallow habit by,
Wherein deep policy did him disguise,
And arm'd his long hid wits advisedly,
To check the tears in Colatinus' eyes.
Thou wronged Lord of Rome, quoth he, arise,
    Let my unsounded self suppos'd a fool,
    Now set thy long experienc'd wit to school.

E

Why Colatine, is woe the cure for woe?
Do wounds help wounds, or grief help grievous deeds?
Is it revenge to give thyself a blow,
For his foul act, by whom thy fair wife bleeds?
Such childish humour from weak minds proceeds,
    Thy wretched wife mistook the matter so,
    To slay herself that should have slain her Foe.

Courageous Roman, do not steep thy heart
In such relenting dew of lamentations,
But kneel with me and help to bear thy part,
To rouse our Roman Gods with invocations,
That they will suffer these abominations.
    (Since Rome herself in them doth stand disgraced),
    By our strong arms from forth her fair streets chased.

Now by the Capitol that we adore,
And by this chaste blood so unjustly stained,
By heaven's fair sun that breeds the fat earth's store,
By all our country rights in Rome maintained,
And by chaste Lucrece' soul that late complained
    Her wrongs to us, and by this bloody knife,
    We will revenge the death of this true wife.

This said, he struck his hand upon his breast,
And kiss'd the fatal knife to end his vow:
And to his protestation urg'd the rest,
Who wondring at him, did his words allow.
Then jointly to the ground their knees they bow,
    And that deep vow which Brutus made before,
    He doth again repeat, and that they swore.

When they had sworn to this advised doom,
They did conclude to bear dead Lucrece thence,
To show her bleeding body thorough Rome,
And so to publish Tarquin's foul offence;
Which being done, with speedy diligence,
  The Romans plausibly did give consent,
  To Tarquin's everlasting banishment.

FINIS

The Phoenix and Turtle

THE PHOENIX AND TURTLE

Let the bird of loudest lay,
On the sole Arabian tree,
Herald sad and trumpet be:
To whose sound chaste wings obey.

But thou shrieking harbinger,
Foul precurrer of the fiend,
Augur of the fever's end,
To this troop come thou not near.

From this Session interdict
Every fowl of tyrant wing,
Save the Eagle feather'd King,
Keep the obsequy so strict.

Let the Priest in Surplice white,
That defunctive Music can,
Be the death-divining Swan,
Lest the Requiem lack his right.

And thou treble-dated Crow,
That thy sable gender mak'st,
With the breath thou giv'st and tak'st,
'Mongst our mourners shalt thou go.

Here the Anthem doth commence,
Love and Constancy is dead,
Phoenix and the Turtle fled,
In a mutual flame from hence.

So they loved as love in twain,
Had the essence but in one,
Two distincts, Division none,
Number there in love was slain.

Hearts remote, yet not asunder;
Distance and no space was seen,
'Twixt this Turtle and his Queen;
But in them it were a wonder.

So between them Love did shine,
That the Turtle saw his right,
Flaming in the Phoenix' sight;
Either was the other's mine.

Property was thus appalled,
That the self was not the same:
Single Nature's double name,
Neither two nor one was called.

Reason in itself confounded,
Saw Division grow together,
To themselves yet either neither,
Simple were so well compounded.

That it cried, how true a twain,
Seemeth this concordant one,
Love hath Reason, Reason none,
If what parts, can so remain.

Whereupon it made this Threne,
To the Phoenix and the Dove,
Co-supremes and stars of Love,
As Chorus to their Tragic Scene.

THRENOS

Beauty, Truth, and Rarity,
Grace in all simplicity,
Here enclos'd, in cinders lie.

Death is now the Phoenix' nest,
And the Turtle's loyal breast,
To eternity doth rest.

Leaving no posterity,
'Twas not their infirmity,
It was married Chastity.

Truth may seem, but cannot be,
Beauty brag, but 'tis not she,
Truth and Beauty buried be.

To this urn let those repair,
That are either true or fair,
For these dead Birds, sigh a prayer.

FINIS

F

NOTES TO VENUS AND ADONIS

References are to the page and line of this edition

Vilia . . . aqua: Let the vulgar admire vile things; for P. 19
me may golden-haired Apollo provide cups full of
the water from the Castalian spring – i.e., from the
fountain whence the Muses drank inspiration. The
lines are from Ovid's *Amores.*

Henry Wriothesley: Henry Wriothesley, Earl of P. 20
Southampton, to whom both *Venus and Adonis*
and *Lucrece* were dedicated was, in 1593, aged 19.
His father had died during his minority, and for
some years he was a royal ward, under the guard-
ianship of William Cecil, Lord Burghley. He was
regarded as a young nobleman of considerable
promise, and he was conspicuous among the cour-
tiers of Queen Elizabeth I for his beauty and intel-
ligence.

makes amain: hastens. P. 21 L. 5

Stain to: eclipsing in beauty. P. 21 L. 9

saddle bow: the arched pieces which form the front of P. 21 L. 14
the saddle.

precedent . . . livelihood: sign of lusty activity. P. 21 L. 26

sovereign salve: powerful remedy. P. 21 L. 28

aw'd resistance: fear of resisting a goddess. P. 23 L. 9

divedapper: the grebe, a shy water bird, which lives in P. 23 L. 28
rushes.

uncontrolled crest: invincible helmet. P. 24 L. 14

there . . . lies: wherein you see your own beauty P. 24 L. 29
reflected.

spring: i.e., downy hair. P. 27 L. 7

moist hand: a moist palm was regarded as a sign of P. 25 L. 23
desire.

footing: footprint – because a goddess is a spirit and P. 25 L. 28
therefore leaves no footprint.

Narcissus: a youth so beautiful that he fell in love with P. 26 L. 11
his own shadow in the water and perished seeking it.

P. 26 L. 18   *get:* beget, be a father.

P. 26 LL. 19–22 *Upon . . . dead:* This is the sentiment of Sonnets 1–17.

P. 26 L. 29   *team:* the horses which drew the sungod's chariot.

P. 27 L. 20   *stone . . . relenteth:* stone is worn by the rain.

P. 28 L. 6   *by . . . direction:* i.e., without being first asked.

P. 28 L. 12   *intendments:* what she had intended to say.

P. 28 L. 21   *park:* originally, a fenced enclosure for deer.

P. 28 L. 26   *bottom grass:* lush grass growing in a damp valley.

P. 31 L. 3   *bid . . . base:* He challenges the wind to play prisoners' base – i.e., to chase him.

P. 31 L. 21   *jealous of catching:* afraid of being caught.

P. 31 L. 25   *swoln with chafing:* puffed with anger.

P. 32 L. 1   *oven:* i.e., a brick oven which was filled with hot coals that were afterwards raked out.

P. 32   *dumb play . . . rain:* all these gestures were interpreted
LL. 29–30   by her tears, as a Chorus interprets the Dumb Show in a play. In many early plays the action was silently mimed before the Act began, the gestures in the mime being interpreted to the audience by the Chorus or Presenter, as in *Hamlet* III.2 or *Pericles* II. Chorus.

P. 33 L. 7   *engine:* i.e., her tongue.

P. 33 L. 8   *mortal round:* the Earth.

P. 33 L. 28   *suffer'd:* allowed to remain hot.

P. 34 L. 7   *in . . . bed:* naked in her bed.

P. 34 L. 22   *My . . . it:* my only feeling towards love is a desire to disgrace it.

P. 34 L. 29   *back'd and burthen'd:* made to bear a rider.

P. 35 L. 10   *press'd with bearing:* overcome by the weight.

P. 36 L. 22   *Fair fall:* good luck to.

P. 36 L. 30   *so:* so long as.

P. 37 L. 26   *crimson liveries:* i.e., the lips' red uniform.

P. 37 L. 28   *infection:* the plague. There was a very bad outbreak of the plague in London in 1592–93 when this poem was being written.

P. 38 L. 6   *seal manual:* impression of your seal.

No fisher . . . forbears: i.e., every fisherman puts back the little fishes.   P. 38 L. 16

world's comforter: the sun.   P. 38 L. 19

Planting oblivion: causing her to forget herself.   P. 39 L. 17

leave . . . commission: takes more than is rightfully allowed.   P. 39 L. 28

Tantalus: Tantalus was punished in the underworld by a raging thirst which he could never slake. He was set in a lake, but whenever he stooped to drink, the water receded from him.   P. 40 L. 29

pine the maw: starve the stomach.   P. 41 L. 2

cold fault: scent which has failed.   P. 44 L. 4

Wat: the hare.   P. 44 L. 7

passing-bell: It was a custom to ring the church bell when a person was dying to encourage his friends to pray for his passing soul.   P. 44 L. 12

leave: i.e., where was I in my argument?   P. 44 L. 25

Dian: The goddess Diana was three-formed: on earth she was Diana, in heaven Cynthia (the moon), in the underworld Hecate.   P. 45 L. 5

forsworn: because she had broken her vow of chastity.   P. 45 L. 6

Till . . . divine: i.e., Diana was angry with Nature for making Adonis as beautiful as one of the gods.   P. 45 LL. 9–10

in . . . despite: in spite of.   P. 45 L. 11

Therefore . . . begets: Here Venus returns to the argument of P. 26 LL. 19–24.   P. 46 LL. 1–18

cabinet: small room. The lark nests in the grass.   P. 49 L. 14

at a bay: brought to a stand round the quarry which has turned to face its pursuers.   P. 50 L. 7

spirit: pronounced 'sprite'.   P. 50 L. 12

strain curtsy: politely yield first place to the others.   P. 50 L. 18

Full . . . effecting: full of notions but utterly careless; trying to do everything at once, but accomplishing nothing.   P. 51 LL. 11–12

all to nought: worthless.   P. 54 L. 3

P. 54 L. 14   *Be wreak'd:* take revenge.

P. 54 L. 30   *Till ... kind:* till the universal (*mutual*) destruction
                of the human race.

P. 55 L. 7   *falcons ... lure:* The sporting hawk (*falcon*) was
                trained for field work by being induced to return
                to an artificial prey called the *lure*.

P. 57 L. 3   *fair:* complexion. It was the high mark of beauty to
                have a pink and white complexion untanned by
                the sun.

P. 57 L. 25   *urchin-snouted:* with a snout like a hedgehog, which
                the wild boar somewhat resembles.

P. 59 L. 8   *tread the measures:* dance formal dances.

P. 60 L. 20   *silver doves:* Venus was transported in a chariot
                drawn by doves.

P. 60 L. 23   *Paphos:* in Cyprus, famous for its Temple of Venus.

NOTES TO THE RAPE OF LUCRECE

P. 65 L. 3   *Lust-breathed:* urged by lust.

P. 65 L. 4   *lightless fire:* showing no flame.

P. 65 L. 11   *red and white:* the colours of beauty and chastity.

P. 65 L. 13   *mortal stars:* i.e., her eyes.

P. 65 L. 14   *did ... duties:* i.e., looked only on her husband.

P. 65 L. 26   *expir'd date:* a state of affairs which disappears almost
                immediately.

P. 66 L. 13   *high pitch'd:* soaring aloft.

P. 67   *But Beauty ... seat:* The idea so elaborately worked
   LL. 1–14   out in these two stanzas is that Lucrece's beauty is set
                forth in her red and white; but the white of chas-
                tity is made red by modest blushes, and the red of
                beauty is made pale by virtue.

P. 67 L. 2   *Venus' doves:* love.

P. 67 L. 4   *gild:* gold and red are often regarded by Shakespeare
                as one colour.

P. 67 L. 8   *Heraldry:* symbolic painting.

world's minority: when the world was young. P. 67 L. 11

niggard prodigal: meanly over-generous; i.e., the P. 67 L. 23
praise was lavish but too poor to express her
beauty.

'*For:* The use of inverted commas at the beginning P. 68 L. 3
of a sentence denotes a proverbial phrase or wise
saw.

margents: margins, where the commentary on the P. 68 L. 18
text was often printed.

than: than that. P. 68 L. 21

His . . . lust: his weak defence of lust, thus subdued. P. 71 L. 20

loathsome dash: mark of infamy. Books of heraldry P. 72 L. 10
include various symbols which were added to the
coat of arms of a man who had committed an
offence against honour.

painted cloth: Painted cloths, depicting stories from P. 73 L. 21
Scripture or classical story, were used as wall
coverings. The figures were often provided with
labels issuing from their mouths which contained
sage or moral sentences.

pure effects: honest purposes. P. 73 L. 27

Narcissus: see the note on *Venus and Adonis,* P. 26 P. 74 L. 13
L. 11.

part is youth: as in a Morality Play wherein Youth P. 74 L. 26
and Old Age appear as characters.

retires . . . ward: draws back its bars. The *ward* is lit- P. 75 L. 23
erally the ridge on the inside of the lock which
corresponds with the incision in the key.

needle: pronounced 'neeld'. P. 76 L. 11

lets . . . time: these difficulties are part of the affair. P. 76 L. 22

cloud: i.e., the bed-curtains. P. 78 L. 7

virtuous monument: recumbent figure on a tomb. P. 78 L. 27

map of death: picture of death; i.e., sleep. P. 79 L. 10

cabinet: small room, tent; i.e., brain. P. 80 L. 22

my will abide: suffer my lust. P. 82 L. 10

For . . . enacted: is regarded as a rightful action. P. 83 L. 25

P. 84 L. 5   *slavish wipe:* mark branded on a slave.

P. 84 L. 8   *cockatrice:* a fabulous serpent, so deadly that it could kill by its glance.

P. 84 L. 11   *gripe:* griffin, another fabulous beast with the head and wings of an eagle and the body of a lion.

P. 84 L. 21   *Pluto ... Orpheus:* Orpheus the wonderful singer, seeking the soul of his wife Eurydice, charmed his way into the underworld. Such was the power of his music that Pluto, god of the underworld, closed his eyes (*winks*).

P. 85 L. 5   *puts ... place:* she often stops her sentences before each is finished.

P. 85 L. 13   *borrow'd:* i.e., guest.

P. 86 L. 15   *be seeded:* i.e., what sort of crop will it yield.

P. 86 L. 20   *vassal actors:* slavish subjects.

P. 86 L. 21   *hid in clay:* buried in the earth.

P. 87 L. 23   *thy ... relier:* lust, which rashly relies on your present mood.

P. 89 L. 27   *taste delicious ... devouring:* This sentiment is expanded in Sonnet 129.

P. 90 L. 21   *spotted Princess:* i.e., her soul.

P. 92 L. 10   *Black ... tragedies:* The stage was hung with black curtains when a tragedy was enacted.

P. 92 L. 18   *proportion'd course:* alterations of light and dark.

P. 92 L. 24   *supreme fair:* highest kind of beauty.

P. 92 L. 25   *noon-tide prick:* the mark on the dial denoting noon.

P. 93 LL. 2–3   *silver shining Queen ... handmaids:* the moon and her attendant stars.

P. 95 L. 18   *Tantalus:* see note on *Venus and Adonis,* P. 40 L. 29.

P. 96 L. 6   *opportunity:* the word means both the occasion and the desire to commit an action, usually evil.

P. 99 L. 10   *retiring:* withdrawing; i.e., if only Time could go backwards.

P. 101 L. 13   *force ... straw:* have no use for arguments.

P. 102 L. 14   *type:* pattern; i.e., wifely loyalty.

badge: device worn by a servant as part of his uni- P. 102 L. 18
form (*livery*) to denote the master to whom he
belonged.

Philomele: Philomela was ravished by Tereus, the P. 103 L. 15
husband of her sister Procne. The sisters in
revenge slew Itys, Procne's son by Tereus. Philomela was afterwards turned into a nightingale,
everlastingly singing of her ravishment.

against a thorn: The nightingale was supposed to sing P. 105 L. 15
with her breast touching a thorn.

death ... debtor: reproach owes death a debt; i.e., P. 106 L. 7
shame demands suicide.

To kill ... pollution: Suicide to a Christian is mortal P. 106
sin – a thought which Shakespeare several times   LL. 8–9
expresses; but by the Romans it was regarded as
an honourable end after defeat or disgrace.

oversee: be executor of a will. *overseen:* bewitched. P. 108 LL. 1–2

For why: because.   P. 108 L. 18

No cause ... spilling: The maid had no reason to P. 109 L. 4
weep except to keep her mistress company.

The weak ... kinds: i.e., weak women are easily P. 109 L. 10
overcome, as wax is impressed by a seal.

fulfill'd ... abuses: i.e., women should not be blamed P. 109
for the lusts of men.   LL. 26–7

counterfeit ... complaining: the imitation of her sor- P. 110 L. 9
row; i.e., the weeping maid.

will: desire – to avoid detailing her shame.   P. 111 L. 11

curious good: elaborately expressed.   P. 111 L. 12

Throng her inventions: crowd her thoughts.   P. 111 L. 14

tenor: summary – a legal term, meaning the sub- P. 111 L. 22
stance of a document.

sounds: deep channels. *fords:* shallow streams.   P. 112 L. 13

Pawn'd ... gage: promised to be faithful by his P. 113 L. 7
bashful looks but not by words.

painting ... Troy: Elaborate pictures of battles were P. 113 L. 23
popular in Shakespeare's day, and the theme of the
great siege of Troy was common. Shakespeare

F*

gives an impassioned description of the sack of
Troy to the First Player in *Hamlet* (II. 2. 466), and
after dramatized part of the story in *Troylus and
Cressida*.

P. 113 L. 26   *Ilion*: the citadel of Troy.

P. 114 L. 2   *In . . . Nature*: more realistically than life.

P. 115 L. 11   *Marmaid*: See *Venus and Adonis*, P. 35 L. 9 and P. 46
               L. 27.

P. 116 L. 8   *strand of Dardan*: the Trojan Plain, surrounding the
P. 116]   city.

   LL. 19–21   *Hecuba . . . Pyrrhus*: see *Hamlet* II. 2. 471–541.

P. 117 L. 15   *the strumpet*: i.e., Helen of Troy.

P. 117 L. 20   *for trespass . . . eye*: because your eye sinned.

P. 118 L. 17   *image bound*: figure fixed in a picture.

P. 118 L. 27   *guilty instance*: appearance of guilt.

P 119 L. 2   *entertain'd a show*: assumed an appearance.

P. 119 L. 9   *Sinon*: sent by the Greeks to persuade the Trojans to
               drag within the walls of Troy the Wooden Horse,
               whence at night the soldiers concealed within the
               Horse emerged and opened the gates to admit the
               Greek army.

P. 119 L. 14   *When . . . faces*: A far-fetched conceit, meaning that
               the towers of Ilion were so high and bright that
               the stars could see their reflections in them.

P. 120 L. 21   *That . . . water*: i.e., as a result of his feigned tears
               Troy was burned.

P. 121 L. 20   *watergalls*: a double rainbow, regarded as a sure sign
               of rain.

P. 122 L. 15   *pale Swan*: It was a popular belief that the swan sang
               for the first and only time in its life just before its
               death.

P. 123 L. 8   *hard favour'd*: plain-faced.

P. 123 L. 20   *Rome*: spelt *Roome* in the Quarto, and so pro-
               nounced.

P. 124 L. 15   *As through an arch*: When the water runs rapidly
               under a narrow bridge, part of the stream at the

edge of the main flow eddies round in a circle until it is again caught up in the flow. Probably Shakespeare took this image from the water which rushed through the narrow piers of London Bridge, especially at high tide. The phenomenon can also be seen under the Clopton Bridge at Stratford-on-Avon.

make a saw: make a sound like a saw, thrust to and fro through a plank.   P. 124 L. 20

Life's . . . destiny: the end of life cancelled by death. The image is of a cancelled lease.   P. 126 L. 21

Brutus: Lucius Junius Brutus was the nephew of Tarquin the Proud, tyrant of Rome, and father of Tarquin who violated Lucrece. Tarquin the Proud had murdered Brutus's elder brother, but he spared Brutus who cunningly pretended to be a half-wit. After the suicide of Lucrece, Brutus dropped the pose and became the leader of her avengers.   P. 126 L. 26

my image: i.e., the child is the father's image in which he sees what once he was. See Sonnets 1 and 2.   P. 127 L. 26

state and pride . . . show: i.e., he drops his assumed idiocy and resumes his natural dignity.   P. 129 LL. 17–18

habit: assumed appearance; lit., clothing.   P. 129 L. 22

set . . . school: become your teacher.   P. 129 L. 28

Capitol: the centre of government, law, and order in Rome.   P. 130 L. 15

NOTES TO THE PHOENIX AND TURTLE

P. 135   *Phoenix:* According to the legend, only one phoenix was alive at one time. It lived in Arabia to the age of five hundred years. When it felt death approaching, it built a nest of spices which was then set alight by the rapid beating of its wings. From the ashes a new phoenix was born.

P. 135 L. 5   *shrieking harbinger:* the screech owl, prophet of disaster; lit., a harbinger was an official sent ahead to make preparations when the Court was about to go on progress.

P. 135 L. 10   *tyrant wing:* bird of prey.

P. 135 L. 15   *death-divining:* foretelling death. For *swan,* see note on *Lucrece,* P. 122 L. 15.

P. 135 L. 17   *treble-dated:* Crows live to a great age, three times (it was believed) the normal human span.

P. 135 LL. 18–19   *That . . . tak'st:* i.e., show your black nature (*sable gender*) in your dismal, melancholy croakings.

P. 136 L. 2   *essence:* essential nature.

P. 136 L. 4   *Number . . . slain:* i.e., they are no longer two but a single unity.

P. 136 LL. 9–12   *So . . . mine:* The image is this stanza is that of two lovers finding themselves in each other. *mine:* golden treasure.

P. 136 LL. 13–16   *Property . . . called:* The two personalities have become so merged that neither can be distinguished. *property:* lit., that which is proper to a person, his individuality or ego.

P. 136 LL. 19–20   *To themselves . . . compounded:* both are now compounded into a unity.

P. 137 L. 1   *threne:* threnos, a dirge.

GLOSSARY

abuse: outrage

accessary: willing

address'd: made ready

admiration: excessive wonder

advance: raise up, promote

advice: prudence

advis'd: determined

advisedly: carefully

affected: in love

aidance: aid

alablaster: normal Elizabethan spelling of alabaster

allow: approve

along: lying at full length

anathomiz'd: anatomized, dissected, shown in minute detail

antics: grotesque shapes

appaid: contented

askance: (vb) turn aside

aspire: break forth

attaint: disgrace, dishonour, infection

attends: waits for

augur: prophet

balk: allow to escape

balm: healing ointment

ban: curse

bane: destruction

bankrout: bankrupt

bars: cogs

bate-breeding: causing strife

bateless: not to be blunted

battery: bruise

battle: army

bawd: purveyor of lust, one who brings the customer to a harlot

behests: commands

beldame: old woman

belied: false

bereft: deprived of

boll'n: swollen

bond: band, fastening

bonnet: hat

bootless: vain

borrow'd: false

bow-back: bent back

brakes: bushes

breaks: is made bankrupt

breeding: on heat

burthen-wise: like a refrain

caitiff: wretch

can: be skilful in

canker: maggot

caparison: harness

champaign: open meadow

character'd: written

chequer'd: speckled, lit., with alternate squares as in a chess board

chest: coffer

chops: chaps, lower part of the cheek

cipher: decipher, read, describe

cipher'd: displayed

clepes: calls
clip: embrace
close: enclosure
close: (vb) closed
closure: enclosure
coasteth: makes up towards
coat: coat of arms
colour: pretext
compass'd: arched
comptless: countless, inestimable
conceit: thought, imagination
conceited: clever
conduit: fountain
confounds: destroys
conies: rabbits
consorted: accompanying
consters: interprets, translates
contemn: despise
convertite: convert
cop'd: encountered
copesmate: companion
cote: quote, note
coucheth: cause to crouch
courser: horse
cozening: cheating
cranks: makes sharp turns
cross-mingle: cross breed
crosses: troubles
curst: bitter
curvets: leaps

danger: power
dazzling: seeing double
deaths-man: executioner

defection: disfigurement
defunctive: belonging to the dead
despite: spite, scorn
diapason: part (in music)
dint: impression
disbursed: distributed, given
digression: fault
dispensation: license to break a law
dumps: melancholy tune

earth: body
ebon: black
ecstasy: excitement
effects: false outward shows
Elysium: heaven
empty: hungry
end: conclude, confirm
enfranchising: freeing
enrag'd: passionate
ensue: come after
entituled: designated
eyne: eyes

falchion: curved sword
falls: lets fall
fancy: love, imagination
fantastic: capricious
favour: beauty of face
fear: frighten
fee: reward
fetlocks: the hairy part at the back of the leg above the hoof of a horse

fine: end
flap-mouth'd: with loose jowls
flaws: squalls of wind
foil'd: defeated
fond: foolish
fondling: darling
for: because
forbod: forbade
forceless: feeble
frets: the bars of a stringed instrument of music
frets: (vb) wears away
forward: spoilt
fume: rage

gage: pledge
gait: walk
gentry: the code of a gentleman
get: beget, father
gorge: stomach
government: self-control
graff: graft
grates: scrapes on
grave: engrave, make an impression on
grey: blue
gulf: whirlpool

hap: good luck
hard-favour'd: ugly
hearsed: coffined
heartless: frightened
help: remedy
helpless: useless
hild: held

impositions: commands
imposthume: boil
indenting: making a curved path
insinuate: flatter
insulting: threatening
intending: pretending
interdict: ban
inur'd: used
inventions: ideas, compositions
issue: child, progeny

jade: poor-spirited, ill-conditioned horse
jealousy: suspicion
jar: fright
jennet: Spanish mule

ken: sight
kind: natural
kindled: reddened, blushing

laud: praise
lawn: fine white transparent linen
lawnd: lawn, open space between woods
lay: song
leaden: heavy
leave: cease
lent: caused
let: hindrance
let: (vb) hesitate
lim'd: caught in bird-lime
limning: painting

lists: places of combat
liver: the seat of the passions
lodestar: guiding star
lust: eagerness

made away: destroyed
manage: control, horsemanship
mated: matched
mead: meadow
meed: reward
merchant: owner
miss: light behaviour
mistrustful: causing doubt
moe: more
moralize: draw a moral from, interpret
mortal: deadly
mot: motto, inscription
mote: speck of dust
mover: living creature
murther: murder
musit: gap in a hedge

nice: exact

obsequy: funeral rite
odd: extraordinary
o'r-straw'd: strewn over
or: either
orient: pearly
orts: scraps
owe: own

pale: fence
palmers: pilgrims

palfrey: riding horse
parling: inviting to a conference
partially: through partiality
passenger: foot traveller
passing: exceeding, very
passions: laments passionately
pelt: assail with curses
pencill'd: painted
period: full stop, end
Phrygian: of Asia Minor
pill'd: peeled
pioner: miner
pitchy: black
pith: marrow
plausibly: approvingly
pleats: folds (of a cloak)
plot: plan
point'st: appointest
post: messenger, haste
presage: warning sign
presently: immediately
pretended: offered
proof: impenetrable armour
prove: test, attempt
purl'd: wreathed

qualified: allayed
quality: integrity
quittal: requital, repayment

ragged: rough
ram: battering ram
rank: overfull
rate: blame

reaves: bereaves, deprives

receipt: what has been taken in

recreate: entertain

recreant: coward

recures: cures again

reek: steam

remission: mitigation of sentence

remorse: pity

repine: dislike

reprove: rebutt

resolution: courage

respect: prudence

rests: pauses (in music)

rigol: circle

rouse: disturb (a hunting term)

sable: black

saw: proverb

scapes: escapades

schedule: summary

seasoning: making salt

securely: without anxiety

semblance: appearance

sensible: sensitive, full of feeling

several: separate

shag: hairy

shifts: tricks

shrewd: ill-natured

sightless: unseen

silly: simple

simple: (noun) drug

sith: since

sneaped: nipped by the cold

sod: sodden, boiled

sort: select, choose

sorts: suits, fits

sorteth: mingles

sounds: swoons

sovereign: supreme

spleen: impulse

spright, sprite: spirit

springing: growing

stell'd: fixed

still: always

still'd: quietened

sting: lust

stories: tells the story of

strife: effort

studded: ornamented with silver studs

stuff up: fill up

subornation: bribery to commit perjury

suggested: prompted

surfeit: feel sick

suspect: suspicion

teen: sorrow

tempering: softened with warmth

tender: grant

tender'd: offered

testy: hot-tempered

than: then

thorough: through

thrall: slave

thronged: crowded, crushed

timeless: rapid

tires: tears in pieces
Titan: the sun god
told: counted
toward: well-behaved, docile
troth: truth
trustless: faithless
tuning: singing about
tushes: tusks

unadvis'd: unintentional
uncouple: loose greyhounds for the chase
uncouth: strange
underprop: support
unlived: lifeless
unmask: reveal
unrecalling: irrevocable

vails: lowers
vantage: profit

vassals: slaves
vent: hole
vent: utterance
vestal: virgin priestess of Diana, goddess of chastity
villain: servant

want: be without
weed: garment
welkin: sky
whe'er: whether
whenas: when
wildfire: 'Greek fire', primitive form of incendiary bomb
will: lust
wink: shut the eye
wistly: steadfastly
wood: mad
wot: knows
wrack: wreck, disaster

AN EPILOGUE
TO THE LAST VOLUME OF THE
PENGUIN SHAKESPEARE

The present edition of Shakespeare's Poems completes the Penguin Shakespeares. The first sixpenny Penguins – the original ten in the orange covers – appeared on the bookstalls in 1935. As soon as Allen Lane realized that his idea was a success, he decided to add a series of Shakespeares for sixpence a volume; and Harley Granville-Barker was invited to be its editor. Granville-Barker declined the invitation but suggested my name – we had recently collaborated in co-editing *The Companion to Shakespeare Studies*. Nevertheless Granville-Barker had a considerable share in planning the Penguin Shakespeares, and we discussed it at length.

There were many problems. The first was the text. Hitherto most popular editions of Shakespeare had been based on the old Cambridge Shakespeare (and its younger sister the Globe). By 1936 these texts were beginning to lose favour, for the bibliographical and textual theories popularized by John Dover Wilson and others had shown to most intelligent readers that the Cambridge-Globe text was neither ancient nor modern but in fact eighteenth-century in form and convention. Something much nearer to the original texts was demanded. Yet an exact reproduction of the First Folio text, however pleasing to scholars, could hardly appeal to the general reader, who is troubled by the old tall *s* which so closely resembles an *f* (and can lead to awkward mistakes), by the use of *u* for *v*, and *i* for *j*, and other Elizabethan practices such as y^e for *the*, or y^m for *them*.

We chose a compromise: the Elizabethan manner of printing a play text, with spellings conservatively modernized, but keeping most of the original peculiarities – the striking dramatic punctuation unless it was obviously impossible, the line divisions, some at least of the many capital letters used for important nouns, but not the use of italics for proper names. On the other side, to omit the often superfluous stage directions and the place-headings added to each scene by editors, who must always locate a scene somewhere (even if only ten lines long), although Shakespeare himself visualized it on the stage.

Further, we decided that each play should be based on one original text, quarto or Folio, but when there were considerable additions or omissions between quarto and Folio – as in *Hamlet* and *Lear* – then these should be included but marked by brackets. Since the original price was sixpence, there was no room for scholarly analyses of variant readings, which indeed are seldom of great interest to the general reader. For the same economic reason the editorial matter was to be confined to a General Introduction, repeated in each volume, giving a short life of Shakespeare and a note on the Elizabethan theatre, and a particular Introduction for each play, giving the external facts needed for a fuller understanding – date of composition, source, text – but avoiding all critical appreciation or interpretation. Notes and glossaries were to be added in moderation.

When we had agreed on these points, Granville-Barker added as parting advice – 'Whatever you do, don't try to be consistent!' This I have found to be good advice, for the Folio itself is a mass of inconsistencies, and not the less interesting for that.

The Penguin Shakespeares appeared originally in a scarlet

cover. The format was designed by Edward Young; and for the only time in my literary experience I was allowed considerable say in the details of setting and lay out. It was a happy and friendly collaboration. Robert Gibbings made a woodcut from the Folio portrait as the only decoration. Shortly after the first volumes had appeared, I wrote *Introducing Shakespeare* for the Pelican series as a kind of General Introduction to the Penguin Shakespeares, and in the chapter on Editing Shakespeare (from which some paragraphs are repeated in this Epilogue) I explained the principles of the Penguin text.

The first six Shakespeares appeared on 23 April 1937, and were welcomed by a party at the Lane flat at 16 Talbot Square by Allen, John, and Richard Lane, Robert Atkins, Rose Macaulay, Flora Robson, and others. The reception was enthusiastic, and two further batches, each of six texts, appeared before the outbreak of the War. Thereafter publication became very difficult because of the lack of paper, but even so from time to time ten volumes were reprinted. The series was resumed after the War with *Coriolanus* and *The Winter's Tale* in 1947; and in the last twelve years the rest of the plays and the poems have gradually been added. During these years also, the first twenty volumes were entirely revised, reset, and enlarged in the new format with the white covers, designed by Jan Tschichold, with a new portrait of Shakespeare engraved by Reynolds Stone.

It is a salutary discipline to edit Shakespeare's complete works from the quartos or the Folio, for which as a text I have a great respect, though my faith in some of the general conclusions of bibliographical scholars has grown somewhat cool. It is a principle, now generally accepted, that when a scholar proposes to edit a play, he shall begin by

taking into account the author's handwriting as mainly
responsible for any difficulties or misreadings in the printed
text. This principle is sometimes called 'scientific bibliography'.

Actually, it is neither so scientific nor so infallible as it
sounds. The modern editor has not seen the original manuscript; he can only guess what its appearance might have
been. Even if it were possible to guess what the printer saw
before him in his copy, the editor must also guess what the
printer *knew*. Most men who write fast and not too legibly
produce in their manuscripts words which are not in themselves clear; but the reader, knowing something of the
matter in hand, can guess the meaning from the context. In
a private letter there is usually not much difficulty. When,
however, a manuscript is passed to a printer who knows
little of the subject and is not particularly interested by it,
he will guess the illegible words; and his guess will depend
on his education and experience. Anyone who has had to
deal considerably with printers and typists will have expe-
rienced this fact. The ignorant typist, unable to read her
copy, cheerfully produces nonsense; the second-class typist
is not content with nonsense, but makes a sense of her own.
The perfect secretary makes a correct copy because she is
familiar with the matter.

My own experience of printers (which is now considerable) has shaken my first faith in scientific bibliography.
The most striking instance occurred in a short introduction
for an edition of Marston's *Malcontent*. Contrary to usual
(and wiser) practice, a manuscript copy was sent to the
printer. The proof returned with twenty-four errors in
2,000 words – an unusually large proportion. Some of these
errors were so striking that at first glance it seemed a telling

confirmation of the value of 'scientific bibliography', but on comparing the proof with the original manuscript it worked the other way. Of the twenty-four errors, only ten were due to misreading of the handwriting. For some the printer could not be held responsible: *Maeilente* for *Macilente*, *Lampateo* for *Lampatho*; *servants* for *seruants*. Others were possible misreadings of the script but made no sense in their context, as *make* for *unable*, *that* for *but*, *pave* for *grave*. The remainder were the printer's own unaided effort, such as *folies* for *follies*, *devision*, *reconizable*, *Johnson* for *Jonson* (twice), *John* for *Ihon* (in a quoted title page), *Parles Church-yard* for *Paul's Churchyard*. Three were particularly striking. I was made to speak of a character called *Tharsicles* in a play of *Troilus and Creosida*, and, most interesting of all, 'they [Marston's satires] pilloried many recognizable contemporaries' became (the printer's mind having strayed from Marston to a motor-cycle for two) they 'pillioned'. Of the twenty-four errors, less than half were due to the copy.

These errors were a revelation of the printer's mind and standard of education. Obviously he was bored with the matter and never gave a thought either to context or meaning. Nor was he used to literary copy. Had he known even the names of Shakespeare's plays he would have associated *Troilus* rather with *Cressida* than with *creosote*; he would have known that Ben's surname was spelt without an *h*.

The handwriting of an author is only one of many causes of error in the printed text, for sometimes compositors will make the oddest mistakes even when following clear type-written or printed copy. In the Penguin Shakespeares, Bully Bottom appeared in one reprint as 'Billy'; 'incontinency' was watered down to 'inconsistency'; while in one proof the spelling 'villian' was consistently substituted for 'villain'. Elsewhere 'Queen Elizabeth' in printed copy reappeared (by inspiration) as 'Queer Elizabeth'! There is indeed no accounting (in spite of Freud) for a large proportion of human errors (including one's own).

Learned editors in theory aim at producing a text which approximates as nearly as possible to what the author originally wrote; but few Elizabethan authors were ever consistent, and dramatists often had second and even third thoughts; Shakespeare himself revised *Hamlet* at least twice. Moreover, no matter how elaborate the critical apparatus or the analysis of the typography and setting, there is only one possible text for the scholar – the earliest quarto or Folio, or a photographic facsimile. Any other edition is inevitably coloured and contaminated by the editor, and therefore unreliable for exact scholarship. The general reader, however, is not concerned with the scholar's problems; he requires a text which is reasonably easy to read and keeps as close as possible to the original, but yet is freed from antiquarian impediments. He needs therefore certain aids to his reading; and it is the editor's task to provide them. There is no rigid principle to be followed in editing Shakespeare's plays, except that the text shall be designed for the needs of the reader who is likely to use it.

In practice an editor is faced with innumerable little problems, each of which must be decided in its context by his own intuition. Spelling is one of the most perplexing problems. Shakespeare's own spelling, if (as is probable) he wrote the passage in the famous Three Pages of the manuscript play of *Sir Thomas More,* was arbitrary and erratic. In one line he spelled More's name in three different ways – 'Shreiue moor moor more Shreue moore'. His punctuation also was rudimentary. In the longest passage (42 lines) in the *More* manuscript, he used 14 commas, 1 semicolon, and 2 periods. A modernized version of the same passage requires 45 commas, 2 colons, 5 periods, 9 question marks, and one exclamation mark!

The editors and compositors of the First Folio text were far more precise in their punctuation. Normally they marked the dialogue and speeches for recitation, and not (as in the modern manner) for syntax. It is a revelation to anyone unfamiliar with the Folio to read for the first time a well-known speech as originally pointed for the reading. In the Penguin text, the original punctuation has usually been kept.

The Folio compositors, however, had their own individual tricks and inconsistencies in abundance, so marked that some experts claim to be able to demonstrate which of two compositors set up any considerable passage. In spelling they will vary between *urgde* and *urg'd*. When it comes to modernizing the spelling, my general practice was to be guided by the sound of the word. *Urgde* is a modern sound however spelt; but *murther*, *burthen*, and *fadom* are somewhat different, and should be retained, although both *murther* and *murder* will sometimes appear in the same play! Some of the Folio spellings are quite fascinating, as when the Clown in *The Winter's Tale* goes to buy *prewins*, which I prefer to the more tasteless *prunes*.

Stage directions in the Folio are often too scanty, and so can mislead the general reader by omitting essential exits and entrances. In *The Winter's Tale* and *The Two Gentlemen of Verona* the copy (presumably the work of a professional writer) was set up in the classical manner with the characters grouped at the head of the scene in which they will appear, but with most of the actual entrances omitted.

Here the reader needs guidance. On the other hand, some of the additions of early editors were superfluous, especially when the action (as so often) is clearly indicated in the dialogue. When Malvolio suddenly interrupts his ruminations to exclaim 'What employment have we here?' it is unnecessary to insert *Taking up the letter*.

Sometimes the Folio will indicate by its stage directions how a scene was played. In *Henry the Eighth, Actus Quintus, Scena Secunda* opens with *Enter Cranmer, Archbyshop of Canterbury*. He is joined by a Keeper. While he is soliloquizing, *Enter the King, and Buts, at a Windowe aboue*. They comment on the Archbishop below, and Henry ends

> 'Let 'em alone, and draw the Curtaine close:
> We shall heare more anon.'

At this point the editors note a new scene. In the Folio (a most carefully edited text) there is no change of scene, but a long stage direction follows – *A Councell Table brought in with Chayres and Stooles, and placed vnder the State. Enter Lord Chancellour, places himselfe at the vpper end of the Table, on the left hand: A Seate being left void aboue him, as for Canterburies Seate. Duke of Suffolke, Duke of Norfolke, Surrey, Lord Chamberlaine, Gardiner, seat themselues in Order on each side. Cromwell at lower end, as Secretary*. After some short speeches the Lord Chancellor says to the Keeper, who has come up to the table, 'Let him come in'. The Keeper goes over to Cranmer, 'Your Grace may enter now'. Hereat the Folio adds the direction *Cranmer approches the Council Table*. On the Globe stage Cranmer has remained on stage for the whole scene. While the table and stools are being brought on, he and his Keeper withdraw to one side until they are summoned by the Chancellor.

Line division is another most difficult problem, sometimes insoluble. Verse is sometimes printed as prose, and
prose as verse. Short lines of verse are common, especially
in the later plays. In the past, editors have often joined them
together to make complete lines of blank verse, rearranging
the rest of the speech. Shakespeare sometimes began a
speech with a half line. This irritated editors, who shifted
the lines up to make them look better, until they came to
some line which would not be moved. Then they left it as a
broken line and started again.

When, however, a Folio text is closely studied it is clear
that much of *Macbeth* was not written in formal blank verse
at all, but in a free, rhythmic verse; so also were *Antony and
Cleopatra* and *Coriolanus*. But readers and even critics have
not realized that Shakespeare often wrote in a free verse,
because they are not accustomed to use the Folio.

For an instance. After the murder of Duncan, Lady
Macbeth and her husband are surprised by the knocking;
she tries to bring him to his senses. In the authorized text the
speech appears:

My hands are of your colour, but I shame
To wear a heart so white. [*Knocking within.*] I hear a
    knocking
At the south entry: retire we to our chamber:
A little water clears us of this deed:
How easy is it, then! Your constancy
Hath left you unattended. [*Knocking within.*]
Hark! more knocking.
Get on your night-gown, lest occasion call us,
And show us to be watchers. Be not lost
So poorly in your thoughts.

MACBETH. To know my deed, 'twere best not know
   myself. [*Knocking within.*]
Wake Duncan, with thy knocking! I would thou
   couldst!

The quick, jerky utterance is much more effectively
shown in the Folio printing:

My Hands are of your colour: but I shame
To weare a Heart so white.   *Knocke.*
I heare a knocking at the South entry:
Retyre we to our Chamber:
A little Water cleares us of this deed.
How easie is it then? your Constancie
Hath left you unattended.   *Knocke.*
Hearke, more knocking.
Get on your Night-Gowne, least occasion call vs,
And shew vs to be Watchers: be not lost
So poorely in your thoughts.
MACB. To know my deed,   *Knocke.*
'Twere best not know my selfe.
Wake *Duncan* with thy knocking:
I would thou could'st.

The editor's worst difficulties come when there are two
or more early texts: a Quarto and a Folio. In some instances
the printer of the Folio used a printed Quarto and made
little alteration.

One of the most difficult texts is *King Lear*. There are
about five hundred differences of reading between the
Quarto and Folio. The Folio text, as a close examination
shows, was set up from a copy of the Quarto most carefully
corrected. Presumably, therefore, the Folio gives what its

editors regarded as the best version. Sometimes, however, the Quarto is better than the Folio and often entirely different. Hitherto editors have simply followed one another, chosing their readings at haphazard from either text, and not always the better reading.

There is a good example in the opening scene. When Lear turns to Cordelia to give her judgement, according to the Quarto version he says:

> but now our ioy,
> Although the last, not least in our deere love,
> What can you say to win a third, more opulent
> Than your sisters?

In the Folio the version is:

> Now our Ioy,
> Although our last and least; to whose yong loue,
> The Vines of France, and Milke of Burgundie,
> Striue to be interest. What can you say, to draw
> A third, more opulent then your Sisters? speak.

Editors choose the Quarto reading, arguing, presumably, that Shakespeare would have chosen the common, proverbial phrase 'last but not least'. Thereby they miss the whole point of the speech. Cordelia was presented as a little creature, physically overshadowed by Goneril and Regan. Lear cannot understand how so small a body should seemingly contain so brazen a heart.

When such problems occur, as they do frequently, an editor can only follow his own judgement. In general he should be guided by principles, but he soon finds that he cannot follow them consistently. He can only comfort himself with the bleak thought that he will have the same reward or punishment as all others who write or edit books. If his work pleases, it will succeed; if not it will disappear. Editing Shakespeare is, indeed, more of an art than a science.

Had this edition been first designed in 1959, I might have altered the plan somewhat; if so, I would have kept even more closely to the basic text, quarto or Folio. The Penguin Shakespeares have now been on the market for more than twenty years, and by the end of 1958 well over a million and a half copies had been sold. It would seem that the original editorial plan was suitable for its purpose.

G. B. Harrison

22   12

22   12

THE PENGUIN SHAKESPEARE

PENGUIN BOOKS